TurboCoach

TurboCoach

A Powerful System for Achieving Breakthrough Career Success

Brian Tracy
and
Campbell Fraser

⁂AMACOM

American Management Association

New York • Atlanta • Brussels • Chicago • Mexico City • San Francisco
Shanghai • Tokyo • Toronto • Washington, D.C.

This publication is designed to provide accurate and authoritative information in regard to the subject matter covered. It is sold with the understanding that the publisher is not engaged in rendering legal, accounting, or other professional service. If legal advice or other expert assistance is required, the services of a competent professional person should be sought.

Library of Congress Cataloging-in-Publication Data

Tracy, Brian.
    TurboCoach : a powerful system for achieving breakthrough career success / Brian Tracy and Campbell Fraser.—1st ed.
        p.   cm.
    Includes index.
    ISBN 0-8144-7248-6
    1. Strategic planning. 2. Success in business. 3. Motivation (Psychology) 4. Performance—Management. 5. Organizational effectiveness. I. Fraser, Campbell. II. Title.

HD30.28.T722   2004
650.1—dc22   2004022389

Printing number

10   9   8   7   6   5   4   3   2   1

Contents

Introduction

In the last few years the field of personal and professional coaching has exploded. Thousands of registered coaches are now working with individuals from every occupation and walk of life. It is now widely recognized that coaching can enable people to dramatically improve their work performance and life satisfaction in much less time than they might ever have been able to on their own.

I have spent my entire adult life researching and studying the most effective methods and techniques for improving personal performance. For more than 20 years I have worked with many thousands of coaching clients. The successes I've helped them achieve are often extraordinary. It is not uncommon for people to transform their lives and careers: to increase their incomes and dramatically improve the quality of their health and relationships as a result of these coaching procedures. Of course, it isn't feasible for everyone to hire his or her own personal coach, and that's why Campbell Fraser and I wrote this book.

In *TurboCoach* you'll find the same proven, practical, powerful techniques and exercises that we offer our coaching clients (who spend thousands of dollars per year to learn and apply them!), and you'll be able to apply them right away to improve your own personal performance immediately. *TurboCoach* will be *your* coach.

With *TurboCoach* at your side, teaching and encouraging you, you will learn how to set standards, priorities, and goals; analyze yourself and identify your personal strengths; delegate, outsource, and eliminate tasks and activities so you can concentrate on the things that are most valuable to you and your company; commit to specific plans of action and improvement; and measure your own success on a predetermined timeline.

With *TurboCoach* as your guide you will be able to achieve the same kind of breakthrough results as our personal coaching clients: achieving balance in your life while at the same time obtaining financial success and independence on schedule.

We invite readers of all stripes—coaching students and coaches alike—to reap the benefits of this turbocharged coaching program. And please let us know how *TurboCoach* works for you.

Brian Tracy
October 2004

PART I
GAIN CLARITY

CHAPTER 1

Create Your Personal Strategic Plan

"Cherish your own vision and your dreams as they are the children of your soul, the blueprints of your ultimate achievements."

NAPOLEON HILL

In the past six months, have you given any thought to setting specific career or business goals for yourself? **YES** ☐ **NO** ☐

If you have set any goals for yourself, do you have a schedule for achieving them? **YES** ☐ **NO** ☐

This chapter examines the critical concepts and skills of personal strategic planning. In the Application Exercise at the end of this chapter, you will identify your career or business goals by developing your own vision, mission, purpose, and skill statements.

YOUR SUCCESS IN LIFE is determined, to a large extent, by your ability to think, plan, decide, and take action. The stronger your skills are in each of these areas, the faster you will achieve your goals and the happier you will be with your life and career.

Personal strategic planning is the tool that takes you from wherever you are to wherever you want to go. The difference between people who use personal strategic planning to organize and direct their lives and those who do not is like the difference between taking a train and taking a plane. Both will get you from point A to point B, but the plane—personal strategic planning—will get you there much faster and without frequent stops.

Skill in personal strategic planning is not something you are born with, like eye color or perfect pitch. It is a systematic way of thinking and acting and is, therefore, something you can learn, like riding a bike or changing a tire. With practice, you can master the many different elements that make up this key skill, and you will get into the rhythm of thinking and acting strategically for the rest of your life. When you do acquire this rhythm, you will realize extraordinary results. Your life and career will take off, and the sky is truly the limit.

Save Time and Money

Why is strategic planning and thinking so helpful? The answer is simple: It saves you an enormous amount of time and money. When you review and analyze key strategic questions and concepts for your career or business, you find yourself focusing on the critical tasks necessary to achieve your goals. At the same time, you stop doing those things that keep you from achieving success. You do more of the right things and fewer things that get and keep you off track. You set performance goals for people and projects. You become skilled at measuring and tracking results. You move into the express lane in both work and life.

The purpose of corporate strategic planning is to increase return on equity. Equity is defined as the actual amount of shareholder money invested and working in the enterprise. Corporate executives use strategic planning to analyze and restructure the organization for the strongest possible financial results. The goal is superior profitability.

Companies undertake strategic planning to achieve better

results by utilizing their people and resources more effectively. Effective planning allows them to outperform and gain advantage over their rivals. They achieve stronger sales, increased market share, better profitability, superior returns on invested assets, and a stronger position overall in their market.

Design Your Life and Career

Your goals in personal strategic planning are similar. The key difference is that rather than improving your return on equity, your planning efforts will allow you to realize a greater return on energy. You might say that personal strategic planning will increase your return on life.

A business measures its equity in terms of financial capital. On the other hand, you measure your personal equity in terms of your own human capital.

Your personal equity consists of the physical, emotional, and mental energies you are able to invest in your career. Set a goal of achieving the very highest return possible on the investment of your energies. You will determine your income and your overall satisfaction by how well you invest yourself. This is the critical focal point of personal strategic planning.

When you are feeling frustrated or dissatisfied or believe you are no longer getting the kind of results you want from your work or your life, it is time to review your strategic plan. This is the time to sit down and ask yourself some good, hard questions. If you are feeling a high level of resistance or stress in your work, or you see that you are working longer and longer hours that are not matched by higher returns, take the time to review and revise your strategy.

Ask yourself this critical question: What is it that I do especially well? Examine the areas where you excel or are clearly superior to others in your field. You need to know what you can claim as your personal competitive advantage.

This is the lifeblood of personal strategic planning. The answer to this question will give you a clear focus in your work and life planning. Your success is tied directly to how excellent you become at the most important part of your work. Of all the responsibilities you face in life, this is one of the most important: to identify that area of excellence that can have the greatest positive impact on your career and your income. Once you know what that is, pour all your energies into becoming the best you can possibly be in that key area.

Gary Hamel tells us in *Competing for the Future* that the top companies project forward five years and then identify the core competencies they will require at that time to dominate their industries. They then implement a development plan today to ensure that those core competencies are in place when the future arrives.

Follow this strategy in your own personal planning. Do you know what core competencies you will need to be at the top of your field three to five years from now? What key skills will you need to have? Do you know how these differ from the key skills you are using today? How can you start to develop these new skills? Begin today to develop a plan to acquire and master those additional skills and abilities you will need to be the best in your chosen field. Then work at that plan every day.

Several years ago, we had a coaching client who was

moving rapidly up the executive ladder. She had managed this in spite of an almost crippling shyness that made her avoid the spotlight. She realized that to achieve her goal of becoming a vice president of her company, she would have to emerge from her shell and develop the skill of making effective presentations. She joined Toastmasters and worked diligently to become, first, an adequate speaker, then a competent speaker, and, finally, a highly skilled speaker. Today she has surpassed her initial goal and is now a senior vice president.

Eight Essential Questions

Here are eight essential questions to launch your personal strategic planning process. Apply your best and most analytical thinking to these fundamental questions. The answers will bring clarity to your search for an ideal business and career.

1. *Values.* In your business and career, which values, virtues, qualities, and traits hold the greatest importance?

2. *Vision.* Imagine yourself five years from today. If your career or business were perfect, what would it look like?

3. *Mission.* Based on your values, how, precisely, do you achieve your vision?

4. *Purpose.* One trait common to all truly successful executives and entrepreneurs is the possession of an ov-

erarching purpose—a genuine desire to serve others through their work or business. What is the purpose of your career or business?

5. *Goals.* To fulfill your ideal future vision for your career or business, what specific goals must you achieve?

6. *Knowledge and Skills.* To achieve your goals and fulfill your vision, in what areas will you need to excel ?

7. *Habits.* What specific habits of thought and action will you need to become the person who is capable of achieving the goals you have set for yourself?

8. *Daily Activities.* What are the specific daily activities you will need to engage in to ensure that you become the person you want to become and achieve the goals you want to achieve?

Remember that the quality of your thinking determines the quality of your life. The more probing the questions you ask of yourself, the more meaningful and helpful the answers will be. Just as there is no limit to how much you can improve the quality of your thinking, there is no limit to how much you can improve your life.

According to the Law of Correspondence, your outer world will always be a reflection of your inner world. Nothing can change in your outer world without a corresponding change in your inner world. The more you know about yourself and your values and goals, the faster you will make the changes necessary for success.

Application Exercise

1. From the list of values found in the appendix at the end of this book, select the three to five values that

most represent the organizing principles of your career or business.

2. Clarify your career or business vision. What would your ideal career or business look like? What would you be doing most of the time? How much would you be earning? What kind of people would you be working with? What level of responsibility would you have? What kind of industry would you be in?

3. Based on your values and vision, define your career or business mission.

4. What is your career or business purpose? Whose lives does your career or business serve?

5. What one goal, if you achieved it, would help you the most in realizing your ideal career or business vision?

6. What one additional skill, if you were excellent at it, would help you to achieve your most important business/career goal faster than any other single skill?

7. What actions do you commit to take immediately as a result of insights gained in this chapter?

"Having conceived of his purpose,
a man should mentally mark out a
straight pathway to its achievement,
looking neither to the right
nor the left."

JAMES ALLEN

What Business Are You In?

". . . Chance only favors the mind that is prepared."

LOUIS PASTEUR

Have you given any thought lately to the question of what business you are in?   **YES** ☐   **NO** ☐

Have you given any thought lately to the question of what business you could be in?   **YES** ☐   **NO** ☐

This chapter examines how to determine who you are and what you want by explaining and illustrating the most important elements of goal setting and strategic thinking. The Application Exercise at the end of Chapter 2 leads you through the critical questions you must ask to begin this process.

SEVEN KEY QUESTIONS AND THEIR ANSWERS—applied repeatedly over the course of your career or the life of your business—can help you focus your thinking and direct your most important decisions. Ask yourself the following strategic questions on a regular basis. A new answer to any one of these questions can dramatically change the direction of your business and your career.

1. What business am I in?

2. What business might I be in?

3. Who or what is my competition?

4. Who are my customers?

5. What is my area of excellence?

6. What are my critical constraints?

7. Where am I in terms of my personal and career development?

This chapter explores the first two questions. Questions three through seven will be examined in the chapters that follow.

Define Your Career or Business Clearly

The first and most important question is: What business am I in? This question is not as simple as it seems. To identify your career or business goals, you must first learn to define your business in terms of what you do for your customer or for your company. Expand the definition of your business so that it is as broad as possible. Never stop with the first answer. Take the first answer to this question and find new applications, new markets, and new definitions for it.

For example, at the beginning of the last century, those railroads that defined themselves strictly as railroads—providers of rail transport—failed to see that new technologies and methods of transport, such as trucks and airplanes, were a potential threat to their business. If they had defined themselves instead as movers of goods and people—providers of transportation—their response to the changes in technology might have been different.

Similarly, in the early years of the Internet boom, many companies operating in that sector defined themselves as providers of free information with a goal of attracting as much traffic as possible. Those companies that failed to focus on selling products or services and making a profit went out of business. They did not see that the Internet is a communication and distribution channel that must be focused on generating revenue and making a profit, like any other business. This failure to accurately define their environment and their business led to the loss of many billions of investment dollars.

When you define your business, think in terms of how your products or services affect or interact with the lives or work of other people or organizations. Consider both existing customers and customers you would like to acquire. When you define your personal work, consider the people you work for and the people you work with. Think about the effect or impact you and the products or services you provide to the organization have on both internal and external customers.

Target the Future: What Business Could You Be In?

The next question to ask is: What business will I be in if things continue the way they are today?

Think about your career or business two years from now, then in five years. If you do not change the way you define your work or your business, what kind of work will you be doing? Is it a sound and viable strategy to continue in your current way of working or doing business, or should you be looking at changing it in some way?

Start by imagining what business you could be in. Where

would a dramatic change in knowledge or skills, products or services, or industries or markets lead you? To express it another way, if you were willing to take stock of the environment for your career or business and commit to taking action, what business could you be in if you really wanted to be?

Take the analysis a step further and think about what business you *should* be in. To do this, take a careful and comprehensive self-inventory. Examine your skills, your abilities, your ambitions, your energies, and especially your heart's desires. Then analyze the market in which your career or business will be operating. Is there a fit? If not, either evaluate the changes you would personally need to make to create the career or business that would flourish in that market, or select a more appropriate market. These questions are among the most important of your life: What changes will you have to make to become the kind of person who can live the life and do the work you would really like to be doing in the future?

Application Exercise

1. What business are you in?

2. What business could you be in?

3. What business should you be in?

4. What business should you not be in?

5. What changes will you have to make in your business to make it your ideal business?

6. What changes will you have to make personally to make it your ideal business?

7. What actions do you commit to take immediately as a result of insights gained in this chapter?

> "Everyone who got where
> he is had to begin where he was."
>
> ROBERT LOUIS STEVENSON

CHAPTER 3

Study Your Competition

"Facts do not cease to exist because they are ignored."

ALDOUS HUXLEY

In the last six months, have you spent any time learning more about your leading competitors?   **YES** ☐ **NO** ☐

Do you have a good idea of what your leading competitors are offering to the market? Are you familiar with their business or marketing strategies?   **YES** ☐ **NO** ☐

• •

This chapter explores how to identify the individuals, both inside and outside your organization or business, with whom you compete for the same results and rewards. It will also help you start developing strategies that allow you to achieve superior results in the shortest period of time. The Application Exercise at the end of this chapter takes you through the steps necessary to identify what your customers are looking for, what your competition offers, and how you can maximize your offerings to meet customers' wants and needs.

• •

COMPETITION IS A FACT OF BUSINESS LIFE, regardless of whether you work for an organization or for yourself. Price setting (either as part of a salary negotiation or a marketing strategy) is a good example. How would you answer this question: Who determines the prices you charge or the salary level you set for yourself? Would you point to your level of sales or your market share, or perhaps your years of experience? Many people would say that their customers or employers set their prices. Others would insist that they set their own prices. In fact, all of these are key determinants of your ultimate professional or business success.

But the primary determinant is none of these. It is your competition in the marketplace. You have competition whether your company sells its goods and services in the open market or inside an organization, where you are competing for advancement or scarce resources. For this reason, it is essential to thoroughly research your competitors and know them as well as you know yourself.

Many people in a competitive situation make the mistake of dismissing the competition. The smart competitor does not look down on the competition, find fault with them, criticize them, or make light of them. She respects her successful competitors and makes it her business to study and learn from them.

Investigate your competitors. What did they do to win that promotion or get themselves hired for that job? What are their strategies and tactics for market penetration and market domination? How do they position their products or services? What alliances or networks do they build to ensure the success of their departments or divisions? Why do people buy from them? How do they service their customers or build relationships within and outside of the organization? What is their pricing policy? What new skills or training do they acquire to stay current? What is their approach to quality control? What volunteer or professional organizations do they join?

Once you have developed an extensive knowledge base and a good understanding of your competitors, look just as carefully at yourself and your own career or business. Identify your area of supreme excellence. What do you do at least 90 percent better than your competition? What is your Unique Selling Proposition (USP)—that one trait or skill you possess that delivers value or competitive advantage to your customers or others in your organization and that no other individual or company can offer?

Once you have determined what it is that you do better than others in your career or business area, look outward. How will you position yourself or your product or service in the marketplace to capitalize on your area of excellence? What sales and marketing strategies will you adopt? Based on competitive pricing strategies, how will you price your products or services?

Maintain the broadest possible scope when you are conducting research on what the competition is doing. For example, if you are in business for yourself, you may find that, in some instances, the competition may not be another individual or company. You may find that you are competing against what appears to be another industry. For example, companies offering land-based vacations are direct competitors of the cruise industry. Both groups compete for the same vacation dollars.

Our goal in this chapter has not been to devise specific sales and marketing plans—we will deal with these in greater depth at a later point. Rather, the objective is to ensure that you are fully aware of the importance of competitive research, have a plan to conduct the research, and are committed to carrying it out. Having focus will greatly increase your odds of achieving your career and business goals.

Application Exercise

1. Who are your most successful competitors?

2. Why do your customers or potential customers buy from these competitors? What advantages and benefits do they perceive in buying from your competitors?

3. What are your areas of excellence as an individual?

4. What are the areas of excellence of your business?

5. What is your Unique Selling Proposition—that is, what do you do that definitely benefits your customers that no other individual or company can offer?

6. What does your customer have to be convinced of to buy from you rather than from your competition?

7. What actions do you commit to take immediately as a result of insights gained in this chapter?

"Great ideas need
landing gear as well as wings."

C. D. JACKSON

CHAPTER 4

Know Your Customers

"A life is not important except in the impact it has on other lives."

JACKIE ROBINSON

Within the last six months, have you taken a good look at who your most important internal customers are? What about your most important external customers? **YES** ☐ **NO** ☐

Within the last six months, have you given any thought to eliminating your low-value customers? **YES** ☐ **NO** ☐

This chapter looks at ways to develop a customer-oriented mentality in your career or business. The purpose is to help you identify the ideal customers for what you offer and develop effective strategies to attract more of those customers to your business activities. The Application Exercise at the end of the chapter will help you to meet the requirements of your most important internal customers, recognize your key current and future external customers, and free up time and energy by identifying those customers with whom you should stop doing business.

CAN YOU IDENTIFY YOUR CUSTOMERS? Do you know whom you have to satisfy in order to survive and thrive in your career or business?

Customers come in two categories: internal and external. The definition of an internal customer is simple. It is anyone who depends on you for his or her success and anyone upon whom you depend for your success. Following this definition, internal customers include your colleagues and your staff. Professional advisers, such as attorneys and accountants, can also be considered your internal customers. In fact, everyone around you whom you help, or who helps you, is in some way an internal customer.

Your external customer is the one who buys what you

produce. External customers are the focal point of all business success. Your ability to accurately identify this customer—the one external customer whose satisfaction determines the success of your business—is at the heart of every element of strategic planning.

Before you can successfully identify this crucial customer, you must answer several questions. How does your customer define value? Can you list the specific benefits your products or services deliver to this customer? Probing deeper, do you know what your customer really wants and needs from you in order to be completely satisfied? Can you say how your product changes or improves your customer's life and work?

The twenty-first century is being referred to as the "age of the customer." The customer is at the center of business transactions as never before. Your success and your rewards in life will be determined in large part by your ability to identify and satisfy your key customers.

If current trends continue, who will your customer be in the future? If you were to change your product or service offerings, who *could* be your customer? If you want to rise to the very top of your field, who *should* be your customer? What expectations will this customer have that you can satisfy by upgrading your knowledge, your skills, and your ability? With the benefit of hindsight—drawing from your current knowledge and experience—can you name any customers in your career or business with whom you would avoid working today? Does your current customer list include any names of people or businesses that should not be your customers?

You can answer this last question more easily if you group your customers into high-value and low-value segments. To do this, begin by identifying and analyzing the characteristics of your very best customers. Sort all your customers according to how they stack up against the best performers. You should be able to see quickly who your highest-value customers are. Today, many companies follow this procedure in order to focus more and more of their time and attention on their highest-value customers and on acquiring more customers like them. At the same time, they spend less and less time on their lower-value customers. In many cases, they encourage their lower-value customers to do business with other companies.

The story of a successful entrepreneur we know illustrates this concept. He recently applied this sorting process to his customer base. He determined that a small segment (20 percent) of his customers contributed a very large share (80 percent) of his sales volume and an equally large share (80 percent) of his profits. His response to this was to "fire" the 80 percent of his lower-value customers that contributed 20 percent or less of his revenues. He identified other companies in his industry that he felt could service them better and handed off those customers, one by one. He was then free to concentrate all his attention and energy on his higher-value customers. Within one year, his business and his personal income doubled. Would this strategy work for you?

Application Exercise

1. Who are your most important internal customers?

2. What are the special requirements of your internal customers?

3. Who are your most valuable external customers?

4. Who could be your external customers?

5. Who should be your external customers?

6. Which external customers are you going to "fire"—that is, which should you stop doing business with?

7. What actions do you commit to take immediately as a result of insights gained in this chapter?

"The shoe that
fits one person
pinches another."

CARL GUSTAV JUNG

CHAPTER 5

Identify Your Areas of Excellence

"I can't imagine a person becoming a success who doesn't give this game of life everything he's got."

WALTER CRONKITE

Can you identify your areas of excellence?   **YES** ☐   **NO** ☐

If you know your areas of excellence, do you know how to develop them to achieve the greatest possible results in your career or business? **YES** ☐   **NO** ☐

This chapter examines how you can isolate and identify your areas of excellence, those key result areas where extraordinary achievement can bring about extraordinary results. The Application Exercise at the end of the chapter will help you to spotlight those areas of your work that tap your highest levels of excellence, joy, and energy.

YOU HAVE SPECIAL GIFTS AND ABILITIES; if you develop them properly, you can use them to achieve all your goals in life. If you are committed to mastering the circumstances of your life, to realizing your dreams, to creating a thriving career or business and leading a fulfilling and creative life, you must uncover these special gifts and abilities and dedicate yourself to developing and sharpening them. Five markers will tell you when you are headed in the right direction on this journey of self-discovery. When you are actively pursuing an area that engages any of your special gifts or abilities, you will find that:

1. You excel at the activity. Your performance is not merely good; it is outstanding.

2. You experience real joy in the activity. You find it more than pleasant or interesting; you revel in the experience.

3. You are stimulated, engaged, and you feel energized. You may have been frazzled and exhausted moments before, but you come to life when you are involved in this activity.

4. Your energy is contagious. Those around you are likewise energized.

5. You are motivated to continuously improve these unique gifts and abilities. You set your own performance benchmarks for these skills, and they are at the highest level. Your motivation is internal, fueled by your realization that these talents, developed properly, will lead you to realize your most treasured goals and dreams.

If we are lucky, we have known someone who has achieved this happy balance of self-discovery and self-discipline. If we have worked with such a person, we are fortunate indeed, because we have had the chance to observe firsthand someone who holds the key to living a truly fulfilling life. Study and follow the example of this person.

You will be truly successful only to the degree to which you recognize and cultivate your special gifts and abilities. Only then will you balance external achievements with a sense of inner satisfaction.

Application Exercise

1. In what areas are you not merely good but excellent?

2. Which of your business activities bring you the most joy?

3. Which of your business activities most energize you?

4. In what activities are you engaged when you notice people around you becoming energized?

5. In what areas of your business do you find yourself most eager to learn and grow?

6. What are the core competencies you will need in order to be in the top 10 percent of your field three to five years from now?

7. What actions do you commit to take immediately as a result of insights gained in this chapter?

"Use the talents you possess,
for the woods would be a
very silent place if no birds
sang except the best."

HENRY VAN DYKE

CHAPTER 6

Remove Your Critical Constraints

"Difficulty is the excuse history never accepts."

EDWARD R. MURROW

Have you identified the critical constraints to achieving your major career and business goals?   **YES** ☐   **NO** ☐

Have you determined strategies to overcome these critical constraints? **YES** ☐ **NO** ☐

· ·

This chapter examines how you can determine the elements in your life, both personal and professional, internal and external, that hold you back from being the person you want to be and achieving the goals you want to achieve. The Application Exercise at the end of this chapter invites you to explore your major career or business goals, the critical constraints to achieving career or business success, and strategies for overcoming these constraints.

· ·

ONE COMMON FEATURE of the complex activities you engage in—from building a production facility to negotiating your daily commute—is that they contain a limiting or constraining factor that directly affects the speed with which you can complete the process or achieve your goal.

For example, construction of the production plant may be delayed due to missed delivery dates or unscheduled soil or groundwater testing. Your commute may involve taking a freeway where traffic slows down every morning at the same point. These bottlenecks or choke points can determine how quickly you achieve your goals, or if in fact you achieve them at all.

To achieve any goal you set for yourself, the first step is

to identify the tasks you will need to undertake to reach your goal. Next, analyze each of these steps to see which is a critical limiting factor—in other words, which of these steps could limit your ability to achieve your goal within the time limit you have set.

Figure 6-1.

Theory of Constraints

Critical Constraints: For every goal or project in progress there is at least one critical constraint that determines how fast you achieve it.

What factor sets the speed at which you achieve your goal?

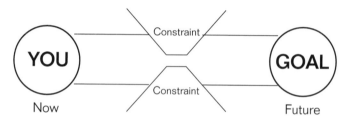

1. Be clear about your goal.
2. Identify your limiting factor.
3. Focus on alleviating it.

At this point, ask yourself this question: Why haven't I achieved my goal already?

For example, if your goal is to increase your income by 50 percent, why aren't you earning at that level? If you want to increase your fitness level, why aren't you exercising every day? Frequently, the simple act of asking and answering these hard questions will spotlight the critical constraint that keeps you from reaching your goal.

Consider this: A small percentage of the constraints that

keep you from reaching your career or personal goals (around 20 percent) exist outside of yourself. The lion's share of these constraints—fully 80 percent—exist within you. The same is true for your business—80 percent of the constraints exist within your organization, not outside. If you have not reached your desired income level, found the time or motivation to exercise daily, or brought your business to desired revenue levels, ask yourself the hard questions. You will very likely find that the answers lie in your own habits, beliefs, attitudes, and opinions, as well as your range and level of skills and abilities—or lack thereof.

Successful people identify obstacles within themselves before looking outside for answers. They ask, "What am I doing that is holding me back?" or "What are we doing inside our business organization that inhibits our progress?" Once you set an important goal, your first step is to start with yourself and look outward from there. You are in control of your own time and your own actions and attitudes, and you must be in control of your own business. Your attitude and energy play a huge role in how far you go in life. Your ability to affect or control other people or external events is limited, so always begin with yourself. Examine each new challenge by asking, "What is it in me that is holding me back?"

Application Exercise

1. What is your major career goal?

2. What are the critical constraints to achieving your major career goal?

3. How will you overcome these critical constraints?

4. What is the major goal of your business?

5. What are the critical constraints to achieving this major business goal?

6. How will you overcome these critical constraints in your business?

7. What actions do you commit to take immediately as a result of insights gained in this chapter?

"Difficulties are things
that show what men are."

EPICTETUS

CHAPTER 7

Where Are You on the Sigmoid Curve?

"Change is not made without inconvenience, even from worse to better."

RICHARD HOOKER

Do you regularly examine your career or business plans to assess their usefulness? **YES** ☐ **NO** ☐

Do you seek new ideas and input on a regular basis to ensure you are responding to changing conditions that affect your career or business? **YES** ☐ **NO** ☐

This chapter examines the Sigmoid Curve, which illustrates the life cycle that all enterprises experience over time. Understanding this cycle can help you to develop effective responses to changes and opportunities in your career or business. The Application Exercise at the end of the chapter is designed to help you master the various phases of growth, decline, and leveling off that characterize all dynamic undertakings.

IF YOU OBSERVE THEM CLOSELY, you will see that careers and businesses follow predictable cycles, like the seasons of the year. Most enterprises follow a cycle that resembles an "S" lying on its side, and this is known as the Sigmoid Curve. All new activities start out at the high point of the "S" on the left, then head downward during a learning phase, head back up as they experience a growth phase, then level off at the top before declining again. (See Figure 7-1.)

The cycles described by the Sigmoid Curve do not just apply to careers and businesses. They describe the life cycles of products and services, relationships, institutions, and the life spans of nations and empires.

Take a moment to assess where your life and your career

or business fall on the Sigmoid Curve. Do you find yourself in phase one, the Learning Phase? Are you in phase two, the Growth Phase? Do you find yourself between phases two and three, in a period of Leveling Off? Or are you at phase three, the Decline Phase?

Figure 7-1. Sigmoid Curve

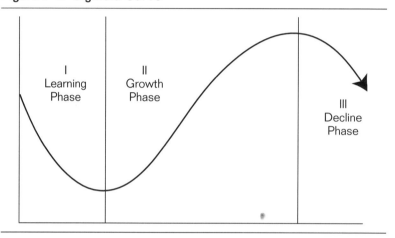

Let's take a closer look at what you can expect to en-counter in each of these phases. Phase one, the Learning Phase, is characterized by a high level of activity. As you launch your career or business, you confront opportunities and problems, take on new initiatives and absorb the lessons they teach you, and invest high levels of energy and time to achieve professional and financial rewards. Most new busi-ness ventures do not survive phase one. They lack either the will or the means to survive, or both. The high failure rate of business start-ups is testimony to the difficulty of phase one.

If you have survived phase one, you will enter the heady atmosphere of the Growth Phase. During phase two, business and revenues surge ahead, possibilities multiply, and the atmosphere is one of energy and exhilaration. This is an exciting time in a career or business when opportunities present themselves at every turn and mistakes are merely chances to learn and grow, leading to new avenues for success rather than failure.

In phase three, the Decline Phase, careers and businesses experience a drop in sales, rewards, and excitement. The atmosphere mirrors the decline in revenues and is marked by a loss of enthusiasm and a dip in morale. The verve and excitement that marked phase two diminish. You may question whether you have chosen the right career, or if you should be in the business you have chosen for yourself.

Successful people learn to track the health of their careers or businesses by continually monitoring their positions on the Sigmoid Curve. They respond quickly and decisively to any changes that could affect their futures or the futures of their businesses.

In phase one, the qualities of courage and persistence help you hold onto the vision you have for your career or business. Flexibility in setting and executing strategy to attain that vision is also a key trait during this phase.

During phase two, enjoy your growing success but keep a close watch on both the economy and the marketplace. Never allow success to make you complacent. Be prepared to make whatever changes are needed to keep your competitive edge. Your first responsibility to both your career and your business is to recognize and understand changes and influences in your market and continually adapt both yourself and your business to ensure continuing success.

While you are in phase two, take advantage of strong revenue and profits by building a substantial cash reserve that can serve as a buffer during this renewal process, which is often beset by unexpected challenges.

The consequence of failing to focus on changing conditions is that change will overtake you and your career or business, and you will find yourself in the Decline Phase. In this phase, old personal habits and business practices no longer work. If you do find yourself in phase three, the solution is simple. Ask yourself the essential strategic planning questions we have examined in the previous chapters. Your goal is to transform phase three into a new phase one by reaffirming yourself and your career or business in response to changing external and internal conditions. The stakes in this phase are high: You must adapt and move on or fail. The challenges in phase three can be daunting, but they offer a chance to expand your leadership abilities, revisit your vision for your career or business, and bring new life to your work. The adaptation and reinvention required of all careers and businesses that find themselves in phase three is a hallmark of life in the twenty-first century. And it is a test all successful people must pass if they are to prevail in their careers or grow a profitable business.

Application Exercise

1. Where are you personally on the Sigmoid Curve?
   Phase one, the Learning Phase?   _____
   Phase two, the Growth Phase?   _____
   Phase three, the Decline Phase?   _____

2. If in phase one, what are you doing, personally, to ensure survival and to move into phase two?

3. If in phase two, what are you doing to monitor the internal and external forces that affect you personally and to continually adapt to any changes?

4. If in phase three, what are you doing to reinvent yourself and move into a new phase one?

5. Where is your business on the Sigmoid Curve?
   Phase one, the Learning Phase? _____
   Phase two, the Growth Phase? _____
   Phase three, the Decline Phase? _____

6. If in phase one, what are you doing to ensure the survival of your business and to transition it into phase two?

7. If in phase two, what are you doing to monitor the internal and external forces that affect your business and to continually adapt to any changes?

8. If in phase three, what are you doing to reinvent your business and transition it into a new phase one?

9. What actions do you commit to take immediately as a result of insights gained in this chapter?

"Business is like war in one respect. If its grand strategy is correct, any number of tactical errors can be made and yet the enterprise proves successful."

GENERAL ROBERT E. WOOD

PART II

INCREASE YOUR PRODUCTIVITY

CHAPTER 8

Eleven Keys to Increasing Your Productivity

"Millions long for immortality who do not know what to do with themselves on a rainy Sunday afternoon."

SUSAN ERTZ

Have you examined the way you organize your time to achieve the best results? **YES** ☐ **NO** ☐

Have you examined the way you approach your work to achieve the best results? **YES** ☐ **NO** ☐

This chapter examines eleven steps you can take to increase your productivity and improve the way you use your time. The Application Exercise at the end of the chapter will help you focus on a critical personal or professional goal and tailor your activities to achieve it as quickly as possible.

PERSONAL PRODUCTIVITY IS A KEY DIFFERENTIA-
TOR between people who succeed in their chosen fields and
those who do not. Individuals at the top of their game have
learned how to achieve more and better results in less time
than most people. Increasing your productivity is a critical
step in achieving your personal and professional goals and
creating the success you envision for yourself. To achieve a
high level of productivity, focus on the following eleven key
areas.

   1. *Develop clear goals and write them down.* Because
higher productivity begins with clear goals, goal setting is a
key component of our coaching program. As you know, a

goal must be specific and measurable to be effective in guiding your behavior. It must reflect your beliefs and be within your power to achieve. The goal and your values must align. Finally, the goal must be time limited. And, to make it real and concrete, it must be written down. The clearer and more concrete you make your goals, the more likely you are to accomplish them in a shorter period of time.

2. *Write a clear action plan.* Next, if you want to turbocharge your productivity, make sure you have a clear, written plan of action. Every minute you spend in careful planning will save you as many as ten minutes in execution.

Create a list of every step or task necessary to achieve your goal. Every morning, write down the tasks you need to complete before the day is over. Always work from a list. Think on paper. This will keep you on track and give you a visual record of accomplishment. You will see extraordinary results as soon as you follow this simple step: The very act of writing out a list and referring to it constantly will increase your productivity by 25 percent or more.

3. *Set your priorities.* The third step is to prioritize your list. Analyze your list before you take action. Identify and start with the high-value tasks on your list. "High value" is identified by the potential consequences attached to doing or failing to do a task. High-value tasks have significant consequences; low-value tasks have few or no consequences at all.

4. *Concentrate and eliminate distractions.* In this step, choose a high-value activity or task, start on it immediately, and stay with it until it is done. Focusing single-minded attention on one task allows you to complete it far more quickly than starting and stopping. When you apply this concentrated attention on a major task, you can reduce the amount of time spent on it by as much as 80 percent.

5. *Lengthen your workday but increase your time off.*
By starting your workday a little earlier, working through
lunchtime, and staying a little later, you can become one of
the most productive people in your field. The early start and
late finish to your workday will allow you to beat the traffic
both coming into and going home from work. This can add
two or three hours to your productive working day without
really affecting your lifestyle. You will derive enormous benefits from these extra hours, which make a relatively small
change to your overall schedule.

Simultaneously, be vigilant about scheduling regular time
off, perhaps starting with weekends. Once you have integrated this practice into your routine, start planning other
short vacation breaks of two or three days. Work up to
longer vacations. When you are away from work, clear your
mind completely of job concerns and engage fully with the
other parts of your life. This will clear your mind and restore
your energy. You will be amazed at the dramatic increase in
productivity you will experience when you are back at work.

6. *Work harder at what you do.* When you are at work,
concentrate on work all the time you are there. Don't squan-
der your time or fall into the habit of treating the workplace
as a community or educational environment, where socializ-
ing is an accepted element of the mix. Rather, at the office,
put your head down and work full blast as long as you are
there. Many people who have followed this simple rule have
doubled their productivity and reached their goals faster
than they thought possible.

7. *Pick up the pace.* At work, develop a sense of urgency
and maintain a quicker tempo in all your activities. Get on
with the job. Dedicate yourself to moving quickly from task

to task. You'll get substantially more done just by deciding to pick up the pace in everything you do.

8. *Work smarter.* Focus on the value of the tasks you complete. While the number of hours you put in is important, what matters most is the quality and quantity of results you achieve. Again, the more time you spend on those higher-value tasks with greater potential consequences, the greater the results you will obtain from every hour you put in.

9. *Align your work with your skills.* Skill and experience count. You achieve more in less time when you work on tasks at which you are especially skilled and experienced. Always strive to become more effective at the most important things you do. Achieving consistent excellence at the most critical things you do is the fastest, most efficient route to achieving the goals you have set for yourself.

10. *Bunch your tasks.* Group similar activities and do them all at the same time. Making all your calls, completing all your estimates, or preparing all your presentation slides at the same time allows you to develop speed and skill at each activity. You simply get better at making each call, writing the next estimate, or designing the next slide. Cut your performance time by as much as 80 percent by doing several similar tasks in sequence.

11. *Cut out steps.* Pull several parts of the job together into a single task and eliminate several steps. Where you can, cut out lower-value activities completely.

Consider the example of Northwest Mutual Life Assurance Company. Several years ago, their system for approving new policies consisted of twenty-four steps conducted by twenty-four different people and, on average, lasted six weeks. Their position in the marketplace was being seriously threatened by companies with a faster approval time. The company consolidated twenty-three of the twenty-four steps into a single job for a single person, who checked every detail of the policy before sending it to a supervisor. In the second step, the supervisor simply checked the analysis of the first person and gave an approval or disapproval. Reducing twenty-four steps to two enabled the company to get the answer back to the field within twenty-four hours, almost always error-free. As a result of the speed of this new processing system, Northwestern Mutual was able to write many hundreds of millions of dollars of additional insurance every year.

The Race Is On

Make a game of it: Challenge your record daily to see how many high-value tasks you can complete each day. Set a schedule and a deadline for yourself and try to beat your deadline. See just how much more you can get done in less time.

Practice visualization to guide your performance. Envision yourself as an exceptionally productive person. For a moment, visualize those times in your life when you were at your peak of effectiveness and productivity. You were doing all the right things in the right way and accomplishing a lot in a short period of time. You felt strong and confident about your performance. You felt stimulated, exhilarated, and in that magical state of "flow" that most people experience all too infrequently.

Imagine yourself five years from now as one of the most productive and successful people in your field. What's in this picture? Visualize your appearance, the way you will be working, the projects you will be engaged in, and the principles that will guide your personal performance. How will your colleagues describe you and your way of working to others? Let these images guide your present performance.

With this vision firmly in your mind, answer the following questions:

■ What are the additional knowledge and skills I need to acquire to dramatically increase my productivity and perform at my best?

■ What are the habits and behaviors that will be most helpful for me to acquire to increase my productivity, results orientation, focus, concentration, discipline, and persistence? Will other traits become increasingly important?

Look for ways to increase your productivity every day. The payoff will be phenomenal.

Application Exercise

1. What are your ten most important goals?

2. Carefully review your ten most important goals. Select one that, if achieved immediately, would have the

strongest positive impact on your life. This is your Major Definite Purpose at this time of your life.

3. What is the deadline for achieving your Major Definite Purpose?

4. What obstacles prevent you from achieving your Major Definite Purpose?

5. What additional knowledge, skills, or qualities will you need to achieve your Major Definite Purpose? What steps will you take to obtain this knowledge or develop these skills and qualities?

6. Whose help and cooperation do you need to achieve your Major Definite Purpose?

7. What actions do you commit to take immediately as a result of insights gained in this chapter?

"No trumpets sound when the important decisions of our life are made. Destiny is made known silently."

AGNES DE MILLE

CHAPTER 9

Pareto's Law

"He who every morning plans the transactions of that day and follows that plan carries a thread that will guide him through the labyrinth of the most busy life."

VICTOR HUGO

Have you given any thought lately to how you can get the greatest return on the time you invest in your career or business? **YES** ☐ **NO** ☐

Do you know your hourly rate? **YES** ☐ **NO** ☐

This chapter examines the distinction between high-value and low-value activities and suggests ways to ensure that you spend the bulk of your time on those activities that yield the greatest return. The Application Exercise at the end of the chapter will guide you step-by-step through a detailed timekeeping process that will give you the maximum return on your efforts.

THE MOST IMPORTANT OF ALL productivity skills is effective and efficient use of your time. Three simple rules can ensure that you earn the highest possible return on your time:

1. Put more time into high-value activities and less or no time into low-value activities.

2. Begin doing new, highly productive things and/or stop doing old, unproductive things.

3. Put as much time as you can into those activities that are important and/or urgent.

Pareto's Law

Italian economist and sociologist Vilfredo Pareto, known for his application of mathematics to economic analysis, developed a key time management concept. In his first work, *Cours d'economie politique* (1896–1897), he published his famous Law of Income Distribution, a complicated mathematical formulation that attempted to prove that the distribution of incomes and wealth in society follows a consistent pattern throughout history, in all societies throughout the world. He proposed that typically 20 percent of the population earns 80 percent of the income and possesses 80 percent of the wealth.

Today, Pareto's Law has been expanded into what is commonly referred to as the 80–20 Rule. Broadly stated, this important principle says that 80 percent of the results you achieve are produced by 20 percent of your efforts.

We have learned that Pareto's Law has relevance to many aspects of our lives. Look closely at your own life. It is very probable that 20 percent of your personal relationships bring you 80 percent of the joy in your life. Twenty percent of your beliefs may govern 80 percent of your attitudes. And so on.

Pareto's Law also has relevance to many facets of business. Typically, 20 percent of your customers will account for 80 percent of your sales. Twenty percent of your products will account for 80 percent of your revenues. Twenty percent of your marketing initiatives will yield 80 percent of your marketing results. Twenty percent of your employees will perform 80 percent of the productive work.

What has all this to do with personal productivity? A great deal. The fact is that Pareto's Law is one of the most powerful principles you can use in your efforts to increase your personal productivity. When applied to the practice of time management, it produces remarkable results.

Basically, there are just four ways to increase your productivity—that is, to generate more results in less time:

1. Do more of certain things.

2. Do less of certain things.

3. Start doing something you are not now doing.

4. Stop doing something you are now doing.

Consider the first two statements: doing more of certain things and doing less of certain things. Pareto's Law makes the task of determining what to do more of and what to do less of relatively easy. It involves four steps:

1. Identify your highest-value activities—the 20 percent of things you do each day that contribute 80 percent of the value of your work.

2. Identify your lowest-value activities—the 80 percent of things you do each day that contribute little of the value of your work.

3. Resolve to spend more of your time on your high-value activities.

4. Resolve to delegate or eliminate as many of your low-value activities as possible.

Applying Pareto's Law in this manner will allow you to significantly increase the level of your personal productivity by clarifying your decisions regarding the best use of your time.

Hourly Rate

One easy way to differentiate between your high-value and low-value activities is to ask yourself this question: Would I pay someone my hourly rate to perform this task? As a simple rule of thumb, to calculate your hourly rate, divide your annual income by 2,000. If you are earning $100,000 per year, for example, your hourly rate is $50. A $150,000 annual income translates into a $75 hourly rate. A $50,000 annual income is equivalent to $25 per hour.

A few years ago, one of our coaching clients, a young woman in the financial services industry, shared with her coach that she spent two hours each morning delivering doughnuts to her clients. She explained that this was her way of letting her clients know she cared. Her annual income was $75,000 and her goal was to earn twice as much. When her coach asked whether she would pay someone $37.50 per hour to deliver doughnuts, she replied, "Of course not! Do you think I'm crazy?" Then she got the significance of his question. Her own hourly rate was $37.50. In essence, she was paying this amount—to herself—to have doughnuts delivered. She decided to hire a student to perform this task each morning and paid him $10 an hour. This freed up two hours each day—the equivalent of more than one working day per week—to devote to her high-value activities. Within ten months, she reached her goal of doubling her income.

You can experience the same positive impact on your productivity by diligently applying the 80–20 Rule in your daily work life, focusing more time and energy on your high-value activities, and delegating or eliminating as many of your low-value activities as possible.

Application Exercise

1. What are your most important business goals?

2. What is your current hourly rate? (Divide your annual income by 2,000.)

3. What is your desired hourly rate? (Divide your desired annual income by 2,000.)

4. For one week, keep a detailed list of how you spend your time. You might use time sheets like those used by lawyers and accountants, logging your time in fifteen-minute segments. This may require a great deal of self-discipline because entrepreneurs think in terms of results, not hours. However, stick with it. See this effort as an investment that can pay enormous dividends. Each evening, carefully review your time sheets. Mark each task you performed with a ranking of one through ten, based on your evaluation of how important that activity was in contributing to the achievement of your most important business goals (highest value equals one; lowest value equals ten). Make a list of all those activities marked one or two—they are your top 20 percent activities.

5. Review your day once again, marking with an asterisk those time slots in which you performed an activity for which you would pay someone your current

hourly rate. Review your day a third time, marking with an asterisk those time slots in which you performed an activity for which you would pay someone your desired hourly rate.

6. Now, at the end of one week of reviewing how you spend your time, make a list that includes:
   a. Your 20 percent high-value activities (i.e., those rated ones and twos)
   b. Activities for which you would pay your current hourly rate
   c. Activities for which you would pay your desired hourly rate

   Moving forward, resolve to spend as much time as possible on your high-value activities—the 20 percent of activities that contribute the most to the achievement of your top business goals and those for which you would pay your current or even your desired hourly rate. Then delegate or eliminate as many of your low-value activities as possible.

7. What actions do you commit to take immediately as a result of insights gained in this chapter?

"The successful person makes a
habit of doing what the failing
person doesn't like to do."

THOMAS EDISON

CHAPTER 10

Zero-Based Thinking

"Most misfortunes are the result of misused time."

NAPOLEON HILL

Have you recently examined aspects of your career or business to assess whether they are worth a continued investment of time, money, energy, or emotion? **YES** ☐ **NO** ☐

Are you prepared to change those relationships, habits, or practices that, had you known when you began them what you know now, you would not get into again? **YES** ☐ **NO** ☐

· ·

This chapter shows how to practice zero-based thinking, a process to help you assess key relationships and activities in your career or business and redirect your energies to support your goals. The Application Exercise at the end of this chapter will help you to identify your goals, examine your personal and professional habits and relationships, and decide whether you are putting your time and efforts into the right activities for achieving your goals.

· ·

HABIT DETERMINES NEARLY 100 PERCENT of what you do. From the beginning to the end of the day, your habits largely dictate your speech, your actions, and your reactions and responses. The connection between our habits and how we live is strong: Life-enhancing, highly productive habits are commonly seen in successful, happy people, while unsuccessful, unhappy people commonly have habits that hurt them and hold them back.

The regular practice of zero-based thinking is one of the most powerful habits you can have. To practice zero-based thinking, ask yourself this question on a regular basis:

Is there anything in your life that,
knowing what you now know,

you would not get into again today
if you had it to do over?

Start with your relationships, both personal and professional. Do any of your relationships represent a commitment
of energy, time, emotion, or money that, knowing what you
do today, you would not commit to again?

Take a look at your career or business. Are you in an
organization or a position that is not a good fit for your values, skills, and abilities? Have you developed relationships or
alliances within your company, division, or department that
are no longer productive? If you are in business, are there
products or services among your current offerings that you
would not offer today, knowing what you now know? Is
there a market to which you are selling that you would not
enter? Are there customers you would not take on? Employees you would not hire? Processes you would not adopt?
Channels of distribution you would not use? Sales and marketing strategies you would not follow?

If you answer "yes" to any such question, another ger-
mane question automatically follows: Why are you still in
this company or in this position? Why are you involved in
this relationship? Why do you still sell this product or service? Why do you continue to target this market or these
customers? Why do you still retain this employee? Why do
you still follow this process? Why do you continue to follow
this strategy? And so on.

No one with a modicum of common sense begins something that does not at least appear to make sense. When we
enter a relationship, hire an employee, make an investment,
or launch a marketing strategy, we do so because we are convinced it will benefit us. Over a period of time, our needs

change. So do circumstances. What made sense yesterday may not necessarily make sense today. Yet often we are so busy that we fail to recognize these changes and, out of habit, we find ourselves perpetuating an outdated or outmoded status quo.

In applying zero-based thinking, you expose these habitual parts of your life. Then you can ask a second question: What am I going to do about it? Often, the answer is to eliminate it from your life and move on. Of course, there may be times when it is not so black and white. In a failing marriage, for example, the wise decision may not be to simply get out, but rather to seek counseling in an effort to solve problems and work to breathe new life into the relationship. However, we have found that it is often wise to eliminate the old, unproductive, perhaps even damaging part of your life or business and redirect your energy to what will work today.

Recall the case of our client who decided to delegate the task of delivering doughnuts to her important clients each morning. This step freed up ten hours each week for her to devote to her high-value activities, and it played an important part in her doubling her income in ten months. Interestingly, before making this decision, she asked herself whether, knowing what she now knows, she would start this practice again. She concluded that this strategy, which she initiated in order to get to know her customers in the early days of her career, now distinguishes her from her competition and, in a sense, has become her personal trademark. For this reason, she decided to continue with the doughnut routine, albeit in a different, more efficient manner—not out of habit, but rather as a carefully reasoned strategy. She is committed to revisiting this decision regularly, applying the tool of zero-based thinking.

This practice of applying zero-based thinking and taking appropriate actions as a result of it requires courage and commitment. You must be brutally honest in your self-assessment. And you must be resolute in your determination to change.

Begin now, and make it a habit to regularly ask yourself the zero-based thinking question: Knowing what I now know, is there anything I would not get into again today if I had it to do over? Carefully examine those activities or elements that gave rise to a "yes" response. Then, resolve to either change them to make them work once again or to abandon them. The results can be quite extraordinary as you eliminate negative, nonfunctional, or even dysfunctional aspects of your life, replacing them with new, positive ones. You will have higher energy. You will enjoy greater peace of mind. And you will be far more productive.

Application Exercise

1. What are your most important goals?

2. Examine your personal life. Knowing what you now know, if you had it to do over:
   a. Are there any relationships in which you would not become involved today?
   b. Are there any habits regarding your health, fitness, diet, or lifestyle you would not adopt today?
   c. Are there any investments of time, money, or emotion you would not get into today?

3. Examine your business. Knowing what you now know, if you had it to do over:

a. Are there any products or services you would not start offering/selling today?

b. Are there any markets you would not get into today?

c. Are there any customers you would not solicit or take on today?

d. Are there any sales methods or processes you would not start using today?

e. Are there any channels of distribution you would not start using today?

f. Are there any employees you would not hire, promote, or assign to a particular task today?

g. Are there any business processes or methods you would not start using today?

h. Are there any marketing strategies you would not start using today?

i. Are there any operating systems you would not start using today?

j. Are there any technology systems you would not start using today?

k. Are there any partnerships, joint ventures, or investments in which you would not get involved today?

l. Are there any business ventures in which you would not get involved today?

4. What actions do you commit to take immediately as a result of insights gained in this chapter?

"We are what we repeatedly do. Excellence, then, is not an act, but a habit."

ARISTOTLE

CHAPTER 11

Effective Delegation

"What we think or what we believe is, in the end, of little consequence. The only thing of consequence is what we do."

JOHN RUSKIN

Do you regularly delegate those tasks that do not represent the best use of your time and energy?   **YES ☐   NO ☐**

Is there room for improvement in your delegation technique? **YES ☐   NO ☐**

. . . .

This chapter examines the process of effective delegation. It is essential to delegate and outsource tasks and activities so that you can focus on the few critical things that are most valuable to your career or your business. The Application Exercise at the end of the chapter takes you through the steps necessary to identify tasks for delegation, choose the appropriate person to handle the task, and define, schedule, monitor, and support the delegated activity.

. . . .

TIME IS YOUR MOST PRECIOUS RESOURCE. The good news is that, in any given day, we all have the same amount of time. Considering this level playing field, why do some people accomplish far more than others?

The answer is not hard to uncover. Every highly productive man and woman understands the importance of leverage—doing more with less, getting more from less—and masters this strategy.

There are many ways to leverage your time, and we will explore each of them over the next two chapters. In this chapter, we will focus on leverage through delegation, concentrating on ten fundamental principles of effective delegation.

Focus on Your High-Value Activities

In previous chapters, you mastered the skill of differentiating between your high-value and low-value activities. You used Pareto's Law and your hourly rate as tools in determining your high-value activities and resolved to focus your time and energy on these, delegating or eliminating the rest. You applied zero-based thinking to identify those activities you would eliminate. This clarity is essential in deciding which activities and tasks to delegate. Effective delegation will free you up to devote more time to those actions that will have the greatest positive impact on your life and your business.

Do What You Do Best; Delegate the Rest

A corollary of the first principle is to do what you do best and then delegate those remaining tasks that must be accomplished. There is a strong likelihood that the things you do best are those for which you would pay another person your hourly rate.

Another way of stating this second principle might be, "Delegate any tasks that can be performed by a person earning less than your hourly rate—or your desired hourly rate." If your goal is to earn $100,000 yearly, for example, delegate any tasks for which you would not be willing to pay $50 per hour, thereby freeing you up to focus your own time and energy on tasks that are worth $50 an hour or more. Any time you spend on tasks of lesser value represents an inefficient investment of your time and energy.

Delegate to a Person with Demonstrated Competence

Having determined what to delegate, the next step is to select the person to whom you will delegate the task. If you delegate an important task to a person who is incapable of performing, you are setting that individual up for failure while setting the stage for disappointment and frustration on your part.

This is not to say the person has to be as capable as you. But he must have sufficient skills and experience to effectively perform the delegated task. Choose carefully. It is in the best interest of the person to whom you are delegating and, of course, in your own best interest as well.

Define the Task Clearly

Be clear as to your intended outcome. What is the end result you want to achieve when the delegated task has been completed? Make every effort to describe this clearly to the person to whom you are delegating the task. Then ask her to repeat her understanding of the assigned task. If her description is not an accurate summary of what you want accomplished, explain the differences in detail and ask her to again feed back to you her understanding of the assignment. If the two of you do not start out on the same page, there is little likelihood of success.

Also, take the time to explain why this task is important. An explanation of "what" you want done without a powerful "why" is dry and devoid of meaning. You want the person to be inspired to complete the assignment efficiently and excellently. This drive will come from her understanding the significance of what she is being asked to do.

Set a Deadline

Set a clear deadline for completion of the delegated task. Do not be vague. An ambiguous target such as "sometime next week" or "as soon as you can get it done" will not serve either of you well. Without a clearly defined completion date, there will be no sense of urgency, and the job may very well drag on ad infinitum, frustrating you both.

Establish Benchmarks

It will be important for both of you to be able to gauge the progress being made as the delegated task is carried out. Specifically, how will you measure this progress? Reach agreement on the yardstick by which you will make such judgments.

Agree on Resources

One important element of effective delegation is to make sure the person has all the resources he will need to complete the assignment in an efficient and effective manner.

You want the delegated task to be completed successfully. Only then will you be able to empower the person to whom you have delegated the task and free yourself up to focus on higher-value activities. Therefore, determine exactly what resources someone will require and then make sure they are provided. For example, if you are delegating the presentation of an investment proposal to a group of prospective investors, someone may require research materials and logistical support.

Discuss this important component of the delegated task in detail, and be sure you reach agreement on what resources will be required. Then take steps to ensure that they will be available when needed.

Agree on Consequences

What will be the consequences of the person successfully completing the delegated task? Are these consequences known by the person charged with the responsibility of carrying it out? Are they important to him? Will they serve to motivate him? The consequences do not have to be enormous, but they should be meaningful to him. Otherwise they will have little effect. Their emotional import is what will have the greatest effect.

Conversely, what will be the consequences of not completing the task to your satisfaction? Are these consequences important to the person charged with completing the assignment? Again, emotion will overrule logic.

Have a frank and open discussion regarding consequences. Be open to suggestions. What you believe to be important to the other person may be a reflection of what is important to you. The important thing is to agree on consequences that are important and meaningful.

Then, when the task has been completed—or the completion date has passed and it has not been completed—keep your word with respect to promised consequences. To break your word is to lay a foundation of mistrust in future communications and projects that will undermine your ability to effectively delegate in the future.

Put It in Writing

Before the delegated assignment is launched, there is one additional important step. Have the entire process described to this point documented in a written agreement. Then, have each of you sign it. Psychologically, this final step transforms your mutual understanding into a commitment.

There is great value in having the person to whom you have delegated the task prepare the written agreement. This is really the only sure way to know that you are both aligned. Do not be surprised if the first draft is not a totally accurate representation of what you thought had been agreed to. Rather than getting upset, you might rather be grateful that the misunderstanding has surfaced now, when it can be easily corrected. Remember, it is your responsibility to ensure that the person to whom you are delegating the task is fully prepared and equipped to carry it out successfully.

Inspect What You Expect

Beware of the trap of delegating a task and then forgetting about it. Effective delegation is not abdication. You took the time to establish benchmarks and timelines against which you could measure progress being made on the project. Use them. Establish a system whereby you will monitor progress by checking on these agreed-to benchmarks and timelines. In this way, you can often catch and fix any problems before they become serious enough to derail the entire project.

There are four final points to be made with respect to effective delegation.

First, what we have described here might be judged as appropriate only for delegated tasks that are relatively complex. In the case of our coaching client described in Chapter 9, who delegated the task of delivering doughnuts to her important clients each morning, such a process might appear to be overkill. Nevertheless, the essential principles still apply. Use your common sense in determining how to apply them on a case-by-case basis.

Second, the degree of competence and experience of the

person to whom you are delegating the task will also come into play in how you apply these principles. In professional baseball, for example, the manager doesn't use the pitcher to pinch hit. That's not his forte.

Third, avoid the trap into which many entrepreneurs fall—depriving yourself of the benefits of delegation because you have no one on your staff capable of carrying out the assignment. Successful entrepreneurs make extensive use of outsourcing. For example, you may spend hours preparing PowerPoint slides for inclusion in your sales presentations, though it takes an inordinate amount of time and you're not even very good at it. Consider outsourcing—delegating this task to an independent contractor who specializes in this area. Your slides will be of better quality, and you will be free to focus on tasks that are of higher value and at which you are more skilled.

Finally, if all of this seems more trouble than it is worth, give it a try anyway. Like any other skill, effective delegation takes time to master. But if you persist, the rewards you will receive in terms of dramatically increased personal productivity may astound you.

Application Exercise

1. What one activity or task that does not represent the highest and best use of your time, but that is nevertheless important to the success of your business, will you delegate?

2. What skills and experience will a person require in order to efficiently and effectively carry out this activ-

ity or task? Who has these qualifications and might be available? The person may be a member of your staff or an independent contractor to whom you could outsource.

3. Have you clearly defined the activity or task you will delegate? Describe in detail the results you expect when the delegated activity or task has been successfully completed.

4. What is the deadline for successful completion of the delegated activity or task? What will be the benchmarks, or short-term results, by which you will measure the progress of the delegated activity or task?

5. What resources will be required to efficiently and effectively carry out the delegated activity or task?

6. What will be the consequences for the person to whom you delegate the activity or task when he or she successfully completes it? What will be the consequences if this person does not successfully complete the activity or task?

7. What actions do you commit to take immediately as a result of insights gained in this chapter?

"When dealing with people, let us remember we are not dealing with creatures of logic. We are dealing with creatures of emotion . . ."

DALE CARNEGIE

CHAPTER 12

The Power of Leverage

"Whenever you see a successful business, someone once made a courageous decision."

PETER DRUCKER

Do you regularly examine other sources of knowledge, energy, money, ideas, and experience to leverage your own skills and strengths? **YES ☐ NO ☐**

Do you know how to build the habits and contacts that will allow you to tap into these critical sources of outside support? **YES ☐ NO ☐**

· ·

This chapter examines the seven key forms of leverage that enable you to tap into a vast network of knowledge, ideas, and experience to expand the reach of your own talents and abilities. The Application Exercise at the end of this chapter directs you to identify and develop these sources in your own life and build a solid career and business network.

· ·

IN THE WORDS OF THE GREEK PHILOSOPHER AR-
CHIMEDES, "Give me a lever long enough and a place to
stand and I can move the world." His words have universal
application. As you will see in this chapter, you too can use
the principle of leverage to expand the reach of your talents
and strengths. By fully developing this principle in your career or business, you can achieve vastly more than you ever
could on your own.

Studying and practicing the principles of effective delegation (see Chapter 11) have given you the foundation necessary to exploit the power of leverage. We will now examine
other forms of this key tool of professional and business success.

Each of the seven forms of leverage can help you expand the reach of your own talents and strengths. Each involves building on the work, talents, experience, and contacts of other people.

1. *Leveraging other people's energy.* The most productive people make sure they have time for the few things that give them the highest payoff by routinely seeking to delegate or outsource their lower-value activities. Chapter 11 covered in depth this crucial aspect of leverage.

2. *Leveraging other people's knowledge.* Applying one simple piece of key knowledge to your situation can make a world of difference in the result you achieve. Finding and applying knowledge from another source can spare you tremendous amounts of money and labor. Follow the lead of successful people and scan books, magazines, tapes, articles, and conferences for ideas and insights you can use to help you achieve your goals faster. Thanks to the Internet, the task of researching other people's knowledge is faster and simpler than ever.

3. *Leveraging other people's money.* Knowing how and when to take advantage of other people's money—by borrowing or otherwise tapping into other people's financial resources—empowers you to achieve things that would be beyond your reach if you relied solely on your own resources. Seek out opportunities to borrow and invest, achieving returns in excess of the cost of the borrowed funds. Among the many sources for funds, consider, for example, chartered banks, savings and loan associations, venture capitalists, and public and private offerings of securities. For entrepreneurs, the best strategy is to develop a solid relationship with a bank from the beginning. It may sound counterintuitive, but the best time to borrow money is when you don't need it. To do this, borrow a small sum, place it in a safe instrument, such as a certificate of deposit or treasury bills, and in a few months, pay it back. If you repeat this process several times, you will have built a solid relationship with your bank as well as a strong credit rating. You will realize the wisdom of this approach to building a strong credit rating on that day when you do need a loan. And, for virtually all entrepreneurs, that day is inevitable!

4. *Leveraging other people's successes.* Study the successes that other people and companies have achieved to gain insights into their challenges and solutions. Most successful people have paid their dues in terms of money, energy, commitment, and even failure to arrive at the top of their fields. Learn from their experiences and study their success stories to see if there are lessons there that can save you considerable time and trouble.

Start by reading the biographies and studying the careers of successful people in your field. As intimidated as you may feel, do not hesitate to seek out current role models and ask their advice. You may be surprised to find that many people who have achieved extraordinary success take great pleasure in extending a helping hand to others who are committed to making a mark in the same field. Advice from high achievers can prove priceless.

Once you have realized your own goals, remember the generosity of those who went before you and extended a helping hand to you. Do what you can to return the favor to those coming along behind you. You will derive unique rewards from helping those who are just starting out, I assure you.

5. *Leveraging other people's failures.* As Benjamin Franklin said, "Man can either buy his wisdom or borrow it. By buying it, he pays full price in personal time and treasure. But by borrowing it, he capitalizes on the lessons learned from the failures of others."

History is marked by great successes born of the careful study of the failures of other people in the same or similar fields. The valuable lessons taken from others' failures can lead the way to better, more informed choices in your own career or business. Watch and listen carefully to the stories of noted failures. Learn the valuable lessons these attempts hold for you.

Listen carefully to the stories of truly successful people. Those who genuinely wish to support you will share with you their failures as well as their successes. Listen carefully to both, but more carefully to the stories of their disappointments and failures. It is here you can often find the real prize.

6. *Leveraging other people's ideas.* A single good idea, developed with passion and commitment, can give birth to a fortune. The greater your exposure to a range of ideas—gained through reading, studying, interaction, and experimentation—the greater the chance you will come across one that will lead you to enduring success.

We are not saying that one great idea is all it takes—just the opposite. A good idea is the very beginning. Stories abound of great ideas that went nowhere until someone else acted on them and reaped untold rewards. Acting on that great idea is the only way to realize those benefits. The idea can be your own or one that comes to light from your research. Whatever its source, the right idea in the hands of a person who is willing to commit energy and resources to developing it can lead to substantial rewards.

7. *Leveraging other people's contacts or other people's credibility.* Everyone you know has friends, acquaintances, and professional contacts. Many of these people can make a positive impact on your career or business. Among all the people you know or are connected to in some way, who might open doors for you? Who can introduce you to people who will help you achieve your goals faster? One key introduction can make all the difference in your life.

In our coaching program, we stress the important skill of asking satisfied customers for referrals. This is yet another important aspect of leveraging yourself through other people's contacts. It is one of the easiest and most cost-effective ways to grow your business.

Mastering these seven forms of leverage will give you a tremendous edge toward turbocharging your productivity. Study and, most important, apply the seven forms of leverage. Watch your confidence, influence, and prospects grow!

Application Exercise

1. How will you leverage your talents, skills, and actions by leveraging the energy of others?

2. How will you leverage your talents, skills, and actions by leveraging the knowledge of others?

3. How will you leverage your talents, skills, and actions by leveraging the money of others?

4. How will you leverage your talents, skills, and actions by leveraging the successes of others?

5. How will you leverage your talents, skills, and actions by leveraging the failures of others?

6. How will you leverage your talents, skills, and actions by leveraging the ideas of others?

7. How will you leverage your talents, skills, and actions by leveraging the contacts of others?

8. What actions do you commit to take immediately as a result of insights gained in this chapter?

"You can accomplish anything in life, provided that you do not mind who gets the credit."

HARRY S. TRUMAN

CHAPTER 13

Ricardo's Law of Comparative Advantage

"Don't try to be great at all things. Pick a few things to be good at and be the best you can."

LIZ ASHE

Can you identify those areas in your career or business where you enjoy a comparative advantage in the marketplace?   **YES ☐   NO ☐**

Are you committed to exercise your comparative advantage by concentrating your energies on your highest-value activities and delegating or outsourcing the rest?   **YES ☐   NO ☐**

This chapter examines the principle of comparative advantage and discusses how to put this principle to use in achieving your career and business goals. The Application Exercise at the end of the chapter leads you through the steps needed to identify your comparative advantage and plan for the most productive use of your time and energy.

A LONDON MEMBER OF PARLIAMENT and stockbroker in the early 1800s, David Ricardo was also an avid student of economics, ultimately succeeding Adam Smith as Britain's preeminent economist. His influence dominated the aims and methods of the discipline throughout the nineteenth century.

A Shocking Discovery

Ricardo is perhaps best known for his theory of comparative advantage of nations, which postulated that specialization leads to wealth and self-sufficiency leads to poverty. Such a proposition was initially regarded as preposterous—and often still is by those who do not truly understand the principle.

Through his research, Ricardo demonstrated that trade between two countries can be mutually profitable, even when one country is more productive than the other in every commodity that is being exchanged. Ricardo used trade between Portugal and England as a prime example. Portugal could produce both wheat and wine more cheaply than England, giving Portugal an absolute cost advantage in both commodities. Delving deeper into the economics of these two industries, Ricardo found that one unit of wine in England cost the same amount to produce as two units of wheat, while in Portugal, the production cost of one unit of wine was the same as 1.5 units of wheat.

Lost Opportunity

Even though Portugal could produce wheat more cheaply than England, every unit of wheat it produced cost the country the opportunity to make a higher profit by producing a unit of wine. This is known as a lost opportunity cost.

From this perspective, Portugal had a *comparative* cost advantage in the production of wine and England had a comparative advantage in the production of wheat. Ricardo went on to show how both countries could benefit by trading these two products with each other, with Portugal focusing on the production of wine and England focusing on the production of wheat.

Application in Your Life

At the personal level, this is why, in our coaching program, we stress the importance of determining your highest-value tasks—the 20 percent of things you do that yield 80 percent of your desired results—and then focusing on these high-value tasks while delegating (or even eliminating) the rest. A second lens through which you have learned to view this principle is your hourly rate. Anything you do for which you would not pay someone your desired hourly rate leads to a lost opportunity cost. As with Pareto's Law—the 80–20 Rule—these tasks should be delegated or eliminated. You have learned that the decision about whether to delegate or eliminate can be based on the rigorous application of zero-based thinking.

Perhaps the greatest challenge in delegating an important task is holding the belief that no one else can do it as well, or as economically, as you. In fact, you may be right. But this is an example of your *absolute* advantage, just as in the case of Portugal's ability to produce wheat more cheaply than England. The answer to maximizing the return on your efforts is to capitalize on your understanding of Ricardo's Law of Comparative Advantage by focusing on those activities that yield the *highest* return to you—in economic terms, the highest net value per unit of work (i.e., your comparative advantage)—and to allow others to do everything else.

This is the key to sound time management and to increasing your productivity. Free up every minute possible for doing those things that yield the highest return on your efforts. Delegate everything that someone else can do at least 75 percent as well as you at a lower hourly rate than you earn or want to earn. This is often described as doing more by doing less. When you diligently apply Ricardo's Law of Comparative Advantage in this way, you automatically raise your level of productivity.

Application in Your Business

Ricardo's Law of Comparative Advantage is equally relevant in the management of your business. To the extent that you invest any of your business's resources—the money, time, and energy of your employees, your physical plant and equipment, your intellectual capital, and the like—in activities where another company has a comparative advantage, you incur a loss-of-opportunity cost. In some cases, the loss can be significant.

Too often, in our efforts to "be the best," we fall into the trap of focusing on what Adam Smith called "absolute advantage." Smith advocated doing all the things you (or your business) do better than anyone else. On the surface, this might appear to make sense. However, Ricardo's Law of Comparative Advantage stresses committing your resources to producing only those goods where you have a *comparative* advantage. You should delegate or outsource everything else.

Consider the case of one of our coaching clients, the owner of a successful company specializing in providing secure investments to affluent senior citizens. He has a team of eight investment advisers and a small support staff. The company's marketing strategy is very specific. It conducts regular targeted direct mail campaigns inviting people to attend a private seminar on investing. The financial advisers conduct the seminars, request that interested individuals fill out a card requesting a personal evaluation, follow up with each prospect, analyze their needs, and sell them on investing in one or more of the company's products. The financial advisers are all expert presenters and are excellent closers. After learning Ricardo's Law of Comparative Advantage, our client decided to experiment. He found an outside firm that specialized in conducting seminars. Although he felt his own team was better, he recognized that the greatest return on the time of his people was realized when they were knee-to-knee with prospects, closing the sale. He decided to outsource half of the seminars to the independent firm and tested the results. Sure enough, although the number of prospects from each outsourced seminar was lower, revenues still increased as his financial advisers were able to devote more of their time to their highest-value activity—presenting the company's products and closing the sale. In short order, he proved to his own satisfaction the efficacy of Ricardo's Law of Comparative Advantage in his business by focusing its most valuable resource—the time of its financial advisers—on its highest-value activity, which is selling the right products to qualified prospects.

Another client's business manufactures a sophisticated piece of medical diagnostic equipment. By the time he entered our coaching program, he had vertically integrated his company with success, and he was able to produce many of the components of the main product more cheaply than he could buy them. When exposed to Ricardo's Law of Comparative Advantage, he recognized that if he were to redeploy his resources, focusing them exclusively on manufacturing and marketing his highly profitable diagnostic equipment but purchasing the components from an independent vendor, he could increase the productivity and profitability of his business, even though he was now paying slightly more money for his components. This is a classic example of stressing your comparative versus your absolute advantage.

Carefully examine your own business. Which of your products and services yield the highest return? These represent your comparative advantage in the marketplace.

Ask the same question about your internal processes. Could you increase the productivity and profitability of your business by focusing your resources on these and purchasing or outsourcing all others?

Application Exercise

1. What are the 20 percent of your activities that produce 80 percent of your results? These represent your personal comparative advantage.

2. What are the 80 percent of your activities that account for 20 percent of your results? These are candidates for delegation or outsourcing.

3. What is your current hourly rate? (Divide your annual income by 2,000.)

4. Are there activities that you currently do that you would not pay someone your hourly rate to do? These are candidates for delegation or outsourcing.

5. Which of your products or services represent the highest return on investment of your business's resources? They represent your business's areas of comparative advantage.

6. Which of your products or services represent the lowest return on investment of your business's resources? These are candidates for outsourcing or purchase from outside vendors.

7. What actions do you commit to take immediately as a result of insights gained in this chapter?

"I know the price of success: dedication, hard work, and an unremitting devotion to the things you want to see happen."

FRANK LLOYD WRIGHT

CHAPTER 14

The Parthenon Principle

"The will to conquer is the first condition of victory."

FERDINAND FOCH

Can you identify the seven core foundational systems of your company or business?   **YES** ☐   **NO** ☐

Are you committed to making small, marginal improvements in each of these seven foundational systems to enhance the overall productivity and profitability of your business?   **YES** ☐   **NO** ☐

. . . .

This chapter examines the Parthenon Principle, which compares the building and maintenance of your career or business to the great architectural creation of the ancient Greeks. It does so by identifying the seven core foundational systems or pillars on which your business is built. The Application Exercise at the end of this chapter is designed to lead you through the process of identifying the key actions you can take to ensure the health and stability of your organization or business.

. . . .

DURING THE PERSIAN WAR, the buildings on the Acropolis of Athens were burned by the invading Persian forces. Following the war, which ended in 479 B.C., the Athenians began rebuilding their city, which culminated in the construction of the Parthenon, the greatest of all Greek temples of the Classical Age. Dedicated to Athena, goddess of wisdom and patron deity of the city of Athens, the Parthenon stood more or less intact for some 2,000 years until the middle of the seventeenth century, when it was partly destroyed in a war between the Turks and the Venetians.

This magnificent structure, the largest temple on the Greek mainland, was supported by more than 150 outer columns or pillars, and it has become an apt metaphor for a successful business.

The Metaphor

The career or business you are building is as important to you as was the Parthenon to the Greeks. It took many years of painstaking planning and excruciatingly hard work to erect this magnificent temple. The same is true of your own efforts to build a successful and lasting career or business.

A level of commitment that was quite extraordinary was essential to the ultimate success of the Athenians' undertaking. No less is required of you.

Like the Parthenon, your career or business is also supported by pillars, each of which is central to its integrity and its survival.

The Parthenon was "built to last." So, too, your career or business must be based on rock-solid principles.

The Parthenon Principle

Imagine the result of a small increase in the strength of each of the supporting pillars of the Parthenon. As each is strengthened, it will affect the robustness—the durability—of the structure. Clearly, a small change in each pillar will give rise to a large change in the overall structure. The same is true of your career or business. This gives rise to what we call the Parthenon Principle:

> Small improvements in multiple areas
> can result in large improvements in results.

Incremental Changes

Consider the human body. It has several systems—pillars, if you will—each of which supports the body. Improve one and the overall health of the person improves. Improve them all by just a small amount and the individual will experience a significant increase in health, energy, and vitality. This is why a proper fitness program addresses all systems: pulmonary (lungs), cardiac (heart), skeletal (bones), muscular, digestive, and so on. As each system is strengthened, the vital indicators of the body's health, such as pulse, blood pressure, respiratory rate, and so on, improve dramatically, indicating a major improvement in overall health.

Similarly, your business or organization consists of several foundational systems, all of which are interrelated. In our coaching program, we consider seven core systems or pillars: sales, services, pricing, promotion, referrals, productivity, and profitability (i.e., cost controls). As with the human body, an improvement in any one of these systems will lead to an improvement in the overall health of the organization or your business. Moreover, such improvements are cumulative. In other words, overall performance will increase exponentially with a change in each area. As a result, improvements of just 10 percent in each of the seven areas of activity will virtually double the productivity and the profitability of the overall enterprise.

Area of Activity	Performance Improvement	Cumulative Effect
Sales	10%	1.10 x
Services	10%	1.21 x
Pricing	10%	1.33 x

Promotion	10%	1.46 x
Referrals	10%	1.61 x
Productivity	10%	1.76 x
Profitability	10%	1.94 x

Focus on these seven areas in your organization or business. Inspire your key employees to do the same. Together, look for ways to make small, marginal improvements. How can you increase sales? In what ways can you improve the quality of your services? What would you have to do to raise prices, even marginally? How might you improve the effectiveness of your promotional activities? What would it take to increase your number of referrals? What steps can you take to improve productivity? What can you do to reduce costs? As the table indicates, if you achieve just a 10 percent improvement in each of these areas, the overall productivity and profitability of your business or organization will double.

Application Exercise

1. What improvements could you make in your products to make them more attractive and salable?

2. How could you alter or improve your sales and marketing strategies and processes to increase your sales?

3. How could you improve your customer service operations to make your business more client-friendly?

4. How could you modify your pricing structure to make your products more attractive and competitive in the marketplace?

5. How could you change your promotional activities to become more competitive in the marketplace?

6. What could you do to elicit more high-quality referrals?

7. What changes could you implement to make your business more productive?

8. What steps can you take to increase the profit margins in your business?

9. What actions do you commit to take immediately as a result of insights gained in this chapter?

"It is not enough to
have a good mind.
The main thing is
to use it well."

RENÉ DESCARTES

PART III

GROW YOUR BUSINESS

CHAPTER 15

Seven Ways to Increase Revenues

"I have always found that if I move with 75 percent or more of the facts, I usually never regret it. It's the guys who wait to have everything perfect that drive you crazy."

LEE IACOCCA

Are you familiar with the seven key ways to increase the revenues in your organization or business? **YES** ☐ **NO** ☐

Have you analyzed the current sources of revenue in your organization or business and implemented the strategies and tactics necessary to drive dramatic growth? **YES** ☐ **NO** ☐

This chapter explores seven essential strategies to increase revenues in any organization or business. It will guide you as you examine ways to increase gross and net sales, explore the profitability of products and customers, and reduce selling costs. The Application Exercise at the end of this chapter focuses on specific tasks you can perform to analyze your sales performance and implement changes to generate higher revenues.

ALL BUSINESSES, LARGE AND SMALL, depend on the generation of revenues for their very survival. Once the money has come in the door, it must be judiciously allocated and carefully preserved in order to fuel future growth. But the first priority of every business must be revenue generation.

In the first two sections of this book, we focused on clarity and productivity, two critical elements of successful career and business development. With this foundation established, this third section focuses on growing an organization or a business, beginning with increasing sales.

Seven Ways to Turbocharge the Engine

To grow any enterprise, you must continually seek ways to turbocharge its engine. You must develop strategies that will drive sales to ever-higher levels while ensuring that your growth in revenues translates into higher cash flow and profits.

Essentially, there are seven ways to increase revenues. Mastering any one of the seven will produce significant results. Success in all seven will lead to dramatic growth.

1. *Make more sales.* The first and perhaps most obvious way to increase revenues is simply to make more sales. Of course, one of the best ways to accomplish this objective is by expanding your customer base.

If you own a restaurant, how can you attract more patrons? If your business supplies parts to OEMs, what strategy will allow you to sell to a greater number of manufacturers? If you run a print shop, what steps can you take to bring more customers in the door?

What new strategies will allow you to attract more customers?

2. *Sell more often to existing customers.* In addition to expanding your customer base, you can also make more sales by selling more often to the same customer. Customer acquisition costs can be enormous. Once you have developed a customer, look for ways to increase the number of times you sell to him in any given period. In addition to increasing your sales revenues, such sales will also be more profitable.

A client in our coaching program owned a small candle manufacturing plant. Her business was profitable but had reached a plateau of $1 million in revenues, and she had been unable to break through to the next level. Her typical customer was the homemaker, and her sales strategy focused on selling candles on special occasions, such as religious holidays. In the coaching session dealing with increasing revenues, she realized she was missing an enormous opportunity as a result of such a narrow perspective.

With a database of more than 10,000 customers, this determined entrepreneur decided to begin a targeted marketing campaign aimed at increasing the number of times each of her customers purchased candles. In addition to emphasizing certain holidays, she expanded her promotional activities to include individual special occasions, such as birthdays, weddings, anniversaries, and romantic evenings with one's mate. Over the next year, she increased her customer base by just 5 percent, but her overall revenues doubled.

How might you increase the frequency of purchases by your existing customers?

3. *Sell something else.* In addition to increasing the number of transactions per customer, you might also be able to sell the customer additional products. Increasing revenues from your existing customer base in this way is yet another example of capitalizing on your original customer acquisition cost.

Ask yourself, "What else would someone who is purchasing my product or service be interested in buying?" The man putting his car through a car wash may be interested in automotive accessories, such as seat covers, organizers, or air fresheners. The woman buying a new pair of shoes might want to complete her wardrobe with a matching handbag. A person stopping to pick up a magazine before boarding a plane could be interested in buying a pair of nonprescription reading glasses.

Consider the case of our candle manufacturer. Might she further expand her business by adding such items as votive holders or potpourri to her basic candle product offerings?

Does the opportunity exist for you to sell additional products to your existing customers?

4. *Make larger sales.* Another way to increase your revenues per customer is to make larger sales. If our candle manufacturer were able to increase the average number of candles sold in each transaction, clearly this would be reflected in higher sales revenues overall.

A haberdashery might introduce more expensive clothing lines, or offer to discount the price of a second suit, or perhaps include a shirt or tie at no cost, if the customer were to purchase two suits rather than just one. A restaurateur might train his servers to emphasize more expensive dishes or higher-priced wines, or offer free coffee with a dessert.

How might you increase the dollar size of your average sale?

5. *Increase your prices.* Perhaps the easiest way to make larger sales is to increase the price of your products or services. The question becomes, how do you justify the higher price to your customers?

The answer is simply this: You must increase the perceived value of your offering. Remember, your competition dictates your price. You must find a way to positively differentiate your offering from those of your competitors in the minds of your customers. You may achieve this by upgrading your packaging or improving your quality control or by any other means that makes economic sense.

Sometimes, the answer can lie in your marketing strategy.

Consider the case of Bavarian Motor Works in Germany. In the 1970s, the company radically changed its marketing approach, positioning its automobile as "the ultimate driving machine." The company spent millions of dollars on a successful advertising campaign aimed at driving this image into the minds of consumers. The company was then able to raise prices based on the new perception of its product.

6. *Make more profitable sales.* To this point, we have covered four ways to increase gross sales revenues. But what is of paramount importance to any business is cash flow and profits. In addition to achieving this end by increasing gross sales revenues, you can reach the same goal by improving sales margins—that is, by increasing net sales.

Examine the profitability of each of your customers. You may find that it varies enormously. Some customers require more servicing after the sale than others. Some have a record of returning products more frequently. The size of the average purchase of each customer will vary. So, too, will some customers purchase more expensive products than others. Each of these variables affects the profitability of each sale.

Also determine the profitability of each product. If you are offering more than one product, you will find that some are more profitable than others. Perhaps they have a higher margin based on current pricing, or maybe they are slower to turn over and eat up capital in carrying them as inventory. You can significantly increase the profitability of each sale by focusing on the sale of your most profitable products.

Do you know the profitability of your individual customers and products? This information can be a key to increasing your net revenues moving forward.

7. *Reduce your selling costs.* We have already mentioned that an important consideration in gauging the financial health and the future prospects for any business is the cost of customer acquisition. Do you know yours?

Examine your sales processes. Do you sell directly or through independent distributors? If you pay commissions, are your commission rates optimal—that is, are they high enough to attract good salespeople and low enough to be practical? Do you support your sales force or your independent distributors with excellent marketing collaterals, such as brochures, catalogs, and the like?

What about your marketing costs? Do you maximize the return on your advertising and promotion expenditures?

Do you have systems in place to accurately track your selling costs? If not, you may be enjoying strong growth in your gross sales revenues but not optimizing the profitability of each sale.

Continually seek ways to increase your revenues, both gross and net. Remember, in the highly competitive environment in which you operate today, there is no such thing as standing still or maintaining the status quo. You are always moving. The only question is: Are you moving forward or backward? The prime determinant of your direction will be your ability to grow revenues and profits.

Application Exercise

1. What improvements could you make in your products to make them more attractive and salable?

2. In what ways could you alter or improve your sales and marketing strategies and processes to make more sales?

3. What additional products or services might you sell to your existing customers?

4. How can you increase the average size of each sale?

5. What would you have to do to justify a price increase in the minds of your customers?

6. How could you increase the profitability of each sale?

7. What actions do you commit to take immediately as a result of insights gained in this chapter?

"I want this team to win;
I'm obsessed with winning,
with discipline, with achieving.
That's what this country is all about."

GEORGE STEINBRENNER

CHAPTER 16

Four Levels of Customer Satisfaction

"It is one of the most beautiful compensations of life that no man can sincerely try to help another without helping himself."

RALPH WALDO EMERSON

Are you aware of the four levels of customer satisfaction?
YES ☐   NO ☐

Are you committed to analyzing your levels of customer satisfaction and finding ways to improve them, with the goal of dramatically increasing both customer loyalty and your level of referrals?   YES ☐   NO ☐

This chapter examines the critical connection between customer expectations and customer satisfaction. Learn the differences between meeting and exceeding customer expectations and what it means to delight and amaze your customers. The Application Exercise at the end of the chapter highlights ways to analyze and strengthen your approach to customer expectations and positions your organization or business to make significant strides in this area.

IF SALES ARE THE ENGINE that drives your business (see Chapter 15), then customer satisfaction is the fuel. Your ability to satisfy your customers is the critical determinant of your success in driving sales and growing your business.

Perhaps the worst enemy of any relationship—be it between two friends, husband and wife, parent and child, employer and employee, or a business and its customer—is unmet expectations.

Have you ever been surprised to come home to an unhappy spouse, or been caught off guard by a disgruntled employee, and been totally oblivious to the cause of the upset? Have you experienced the wrath of an angry customer and been at a loss as to what went wrong? You're not alone. Such experiences are common. What few people understand is that very frequently, the displeasure of the spouse or employee or customer was rooted in another person not meeting some expectation—an expectation that they had failed to recognize. At the very least, such unmet expectations result in friction. At worst, they can end the relationship.

The Four Levels of Customer Satisfaction

There are four levels of customer satisfaction, all based on the degree to which you meet customer expectations. The higher the level you achieve, the more you will build customer loyalty and the greater will be your success.

Meet Customer Expectations

The minimum requirement to simply stay in business—to survive—is to meet the expectations of your customers. At this level, your customers have no complaints. They are satisfied for the moment. But they are not loyal. If a competitor demonstrates that it can and will do more than merely meet their expectations, your customers will very quickly become ex-customers. Moreover, if you fail to meet their expectations, perhaps only one time, they will leave and find someone else who will.

It can be instructive to observe your local merchants—true entrepreneurs. One of our clients shared the following experience.

There are four dry cleaners in her neighborhood, and for several years she had frequented one exclusively. Twice a week, she would drop off her family's cleaning in the morning and pick it up that evening. Although there were frequent changes in personnel, with some employees friendlier than others, her clothes were always ready the same day. As a busy working wife and mother, this was important to her and, although she often received flyers from other dry cleaners offering cheaper service, she felt no compulsion to even try them out. Once when she stopped in to pick up her cleaning at the end of a hectic day, the proprietor explained they had been very busy and her clothes would not be ready until the next day. She said nothing but, on the way home, she stopped at a nearby competitor and asked if they had same-day service. They did, and that was all it took for her to switch. She picked up her clothes at her old dry cleaner the following evening and never returned. Over the years, she had come to expect same-day service. All it took was a single experience of unmet expectations for her dry cleaner to lose a valuable customer.

What do your customers expect of you? You should be very clear about this. And you must make every effort to at least meet these expectations.

Exceed Customer Expectations

This higher level of customer satisfaction is reached by surprising your customers, going beyond what they expected. Fast, friendly service, followed up by a phone call to make sure everything is all right, might put you into this category. So does a product or service that is a cut above that of your competitors.

Another client shared the following story. As a youngster, he joined his father every Saturday in what became a father-son ritual. Early in the morning, before the rest of the family awoke, they drove across town and picked up a dozen doughnuts, a treat that they relished. As he grew older, he noticed that they drove past several doughnut shops, but always added several miles to their trip to go to the same shop. When he asked his father why they didn't buy from a shop closer to home—after all, he reasoned, doughnuts are doughnuts, regardless of where you buy them—his dad explained that his favorite shop had a practice of adding an extra free doughnut to the box each time they purchased a dozen (also known as "a baker's dozen"). Our client somewhat sheepishly shared that the ritual has been passed to the next generation. He and his son continue to frequent the same shop on the far side of town!

This second level of customer service moves you beyond mere survival, building a measure of customer loyalty and giving you an edge over your competitors. It can also increase your profitability. Customers who experience the kind of service that exceeds their expectations are often willing to pay for it, enabling the supplier to raise prices and thus improve profit margins.

Think of those times your own expectations have been exceeded. How did it make you feel? What was your attitude to this company? How might you exceed the expectations of your customers?

Delight Your Customers

Have you ever experienced a level of service that not only exceeded your expectations, but actually brought a smile to your face? A customer served at this level is truly delighted. Not only have the customers' basic needs been met or even exceeded, but they have truly been touched on an emotional level. And once customers have enjoyed this experience, it will be very difficult for a competitor to pry them away. When you delight your customers, you are on the way to creating an exceptional and highly profitable business.

There are countless cost-effective ways to delight your customers. Consider the difference between first-class and coach service on most airlines. Some passengers are willing—are delighted—to pay two and three times as much for a little extra leg room and free cocktails. One airline delights all its passengers by having its flight attendants deliver the standard dry announcements with humor. A law firm whose clients are all in the medical supplies field insists that all of its lawyers subscribe to and read the leading journals in the industry it serves. Clients are often delighted to receive an article from their attorney that relates to an important initiative they are in the process of launching.

To delight your customer is to show that you care—truly care—about him. No wonder it brings a smile to his face! The greater your success in delighting your customers, the greater success you will enjoy in your business.

Amaze Your Customers

This fourth level of customer satisfaction is what will propel your business into the stratosphere. It requires you to not just meet or exceed your customers' expectations, nor to simply delight them, but to truly amaze them. When you are able to accomplish this on a regular basis, you will be in a position to dominate the marketplace and achieve remarkable rates of revenue growth and profitability.

One of our clients is an orthopedic surgeon who regularly

amazes his customers. He performs many arthroscopic procedures on an outpatient basis and, when the patient (i.e., customer) arrives at the hospital, she is treated like the special person she is. A charming woman trained in customer service shows her into a comfortable private waiting room and offers her an array of current reading material, including the morning newspaper. Normally, patients are accompanied by a friend or family member who is treated in the same friendly manner. Next, a nurse comes in and addresses any questions or concerns either of them may have. While the patient is undergoing the surgical procedure, her companion is offered an array of juices, coffee, tea, and pastries. Within a few hours of being discharged, the patient receives a phone call from a nurse at the doctor's office inquiring how she is doing and whether she has any needs. She receives a similar call each day for anywhere from two days to one week, depending on the nature of the surgery. After ten days, she receives a card signed personally by the surgeon.

Have you ever been treated this way by your doctor? Do you think our client succeeds in amazing his customers? If his patient requires additional orthopedic work in the future, whom do you think she will call? If one of her friends requires the services of an orthopedic surgeon, whom do you think she will recommend?

Examine your business. How might you amaze your customers? The only limit is your own imagination.

Clearly, one key to growing your business—to increasing revenues and enhancing profit margins—is to continually seek to improve the level of customer satisfaction with your products and services. At the very least, be sure that you meet and preferably exceed your customers' expectations. If you want extraordinary results, find ways to delight your customers. And if your goal is to lead in your field and dominate your market, focus on ways to amaze your customers. This will lead to unparalleled customer loyalty and to a torrent of referrals—a subject we will explore in more depth in the next chapter.

Application Exercise

1. What do your customers expect when they purchase your products or services?

2. Do you consistently meet these expectations?

3. If you do not consistently meet your customers' expectations, what steps will you take to ensure you will meet them moving forward?

4. How could you exceed your customers' expectations?

5. How could you delight your customers?

6. How could you amaze your customers?

7. What actions do you commit to take immediately as a result of insights gained in this chapter?

"It takes twenty years to build a reputation and five minutes to lose it."

WARREN BUFFETT

CHAPTER 17

Build Your Business Through Referrals

"Nothing great has ever been achieved except by those who dared believe something inside them was superior to circumstances."

BRUCE BARTON

Do you have a sound strategy in place for creating a "golden chain" of referrals for your organization or business?   **YES** ☐   **NO** ☐

Have you examined your practices for creating and keeping customers, serving their needs, monitoring word of mouth, asking for referrals, and thanking customers?   **YES** ☐   **NO** ☐

This chapter explores the strategies and techniques necessary to build a golden chain of referrals for your organization or business. Examine how to develop customers who will help build your organization or business through referrals. Learn how your approach to creating and keeping new customers, delivering customer service, fostering strong word of mouth, asking for referrals, and thanking customers can dramatically affect your sales and marketing efforts. The Application Exercise at the end of this chapter focuses on key questions to ask in order to build your base of customer referrals.

THE HIGHER YOU RISE on the customer satisfaction scale, the more success you will achieve. The aim of every business is to reach the fourth level, where it continually amazes its customers.

Why? It's simple: Your job as an executive or entrepreneur is to create and keep customers. The highest level of customer satisfaction will enable you to do just that.

Today's business climate is ever more competitive, and customer acquisition costs—that is, the price you pay to generate new customers—are increasing at a rapid rate. Sales and marketing budgets can consume an inordinate amount of cash. Prospecting and cold calling can consume an enormous amount of time. For this reason, a customer who is referred to you by an existing satisfied customer is a jewel to be sought and treasured.

A major hurdle in the selling process is that of earning the trust of a prospective customer. When you have been referred by someone the prospect trusts, you inherit part of that trust. As a result, you stand a much better chance of getting in the door. You will also be much more likely to move through the sales process quickly, as the rapport-building stage will be far easier and the objections far fewer. And at the end of your presentation, it will be far easier to close the sale. In fact, it is often said that a good referral is fifteen times easier to sell to than a cold call.

To gain a huge competitive advantage, to assure yourself of a jump-start in growing your business, commit yourself to devising a sound strategy for developing a "golden chain" of referrals. Your goal should be to reach the point where you never have to cold call again, where you sell by referral only.

Your most likely source of referrals is your existing client base—specifically those customers who are delighted or amazed with your product or service and therefore represent the highest levels of customer satisfaction.

Keeping Customers

Just as a referral is fifteen times easier to sell to than is a cold call, it is said that a satisfied customer is ten times easier to sell to than is a new customer. At the other end of the spectrum, a study by the White House Office of Consumer Affairs discovered that 90 percent of dissatisfied customers will not do business with that company again.

In other words, there is a very real and tangible benefit in making sure that you retain your existing customers.

Not only is the "delighted" or "amazed" customer the best source of referrals, she is also highly likely to be a repeat customer. Rarely will a person who has reached this level of satisfaction with you, your company, your people, and your product or service jump ship and move to another supplier. In psychological terms, people move away from pain and toward pleasure. A satisfied customer already experiences pleasure dealing with you and your company. A move to one of your competitors represents a risk of possibly experiencing pain, if only because of all the unknowns involved in such a change. Will the product work as well as yours? Will it be as reliable in yielding predictable results? Will the after-service be as dependable? Will the customer enjoy interacting with your competitor and its people as much as with you and your team?

There is an axiom well known to the expert bridge player: "When in doubt, pass." This same principle governs the behavior of customers. When they are highly satisfied with your product and service, why risk switching? In most cases, even when presented with a persuasive argument by your competitor, the highly satisfied customer will pass. He will remain loyal to you and buy from you over and over again. This is your goal.

Customer Service:
A Key to Customer Satisfaction

Clearly, you must make every effort to ensure the highest level of customer satisfaction possible. In Chapter 16, we fo-

cused on developing strategies to move your customers up
the continuum from merely meeting or exceeding customer
expectations to delighting and even amazing them. Revisit
and revise these strategies regularly. Strategies that work
today may be outmoded or copied tomorrow. They must be
continually revisited and frequently revised.

Customer service is an important key to ensuring customer satisfaction and, therefore, to attracting and retaining
customers. In fact, it is said that the sale begins when the
customer says, "Yes."

It is not unusual for a customer to go through an emotional dip after the sale is closed. Typically, the time of sale
represents a "high," as the customer looks forward to enjoying the benefits promised by your product. Shortly, however,
he may begin to question his decision, perhaps wondering
whether he might have found a less expensive provider, or
whether the product will perform up to his expectations, or
whether he even needs the product at all, and so on. You
need to recognize that this "buyer's remorse" is normal and
predictable, and then make every effort to move the customer
through this phase.

One way to reassure your customer that he has made a
wise decision, to remove any lingering doubts with respect to
his decision to purchase your product, is to be extraordi-
narily responsive to his needs after the sale has closed.

A brief thank-you note immediately after the sale—even
after each call during the sales process—helps lock in the
sale.

A follow-up call to check on his experience with your
product is a strong signal that you care—not about the sale,
but about him!

If you receive a message that your customer has called

with a question or concern, respond quickly. This will reinforce in his mind that you are committed to his complete satisfaction with your product.

Your total commitment to customer service is absolutely essential in creating customer satisfaction and customer loyalty. This is the first step in the process of establishing repeat business and the foundation upon which to build a powerful referral system.

The Power of Word of Mouth

One of the most powerful determinants of the future success of your business is the little understood phenomenon of word-of-mouth communication. In his book, *The World's Best Known Marketing Secret,* Ivan R. Misner refers to this as the "W-O-M Factor."

Earlier, we noted that fully 90 percent of dissatisfied customers will not do business again with the company that fails to meet their expectations. The same study also concluded that, on average, each dissatisfied customer will share his dissatisfaction with at least nine other people. A similar study conducted by an independent market research firm found that each of these nine people is likely to tell five other people. What this means is that the dissatisfaction of just one disgruntled customer ends up poisoning the minds of forty-five other people.

What company can afford such adverse publicity? Yet, without a well-thought-out customer service program—and a relentless commitment to its application—there is good chance that this will be exactly what occurs.

Creating a "Golden Chain" of Referrals

It is often argued that the inverse is also true: A satisfied customer will share his "delight" or "amazement" with nine of his friends and relatives and associates, who will in turn pass the good news on to five others. Unfortunately, studies show otherwise. In his book *Word-of-Mouth Marketing,* Jerry Wilson claims that the number of customers who will tell a positive story of their experience with you or your company or your product is one-tenth of the number who will share a negative story.

In other words, while excellent customer service is essential in reducing or even eliminating negative word of mouth, you cannot rely on positive word of mouth to produce a stream of referrals. Building a satisfied and loyal customer base is certainly the first step. But more is required. Next, you must design a workable referral plan.

Asking for Referrals

Referrals do not just happen. Have you ever answered your phone and heard the party on the other end of the line say, "Hi, this is Shirley calling. A friend of mine is a client of yours and she recommended I call you about . . . (your product). Would you be willing to meet with me?" Although this would be wonderful, it rarely happens. Waiting for the phone to ring is a lousy marketing strategy!

If you are to build a pipeline of referrals, you must create it yourself. This means you must ask for them. That's right—ask!

And the most productive source of referrals to start with is your existing customer or prospect list.

Asking for Referrals in Advance of Selling

Early in the closing process, before asking for the sale, you might say this to a new prospect: "Although I believe you will find our product is exactly what you need, I know it's not for everyone. If you find my offering attractive, even if you don't personally have a need for it at this time, would you be willing to introduce me to someone you know who does?" Provided you have built trust with your prospect, there is a strong likelihood he will agree.

Should this sale in fact not take place, again ask for names and contact information. If your customer provides one, do not hesitate to say, "Thank you so much. I assure you I will treat your friend with the same care and respect I have shown you. Do you know anyone else you might recommend?" Always attempt to leave with two or three referrals.

In this way, you can ensure that a lost sale is not a lost opportunity.

Asking for Referrals After the Closing

We have pointed out that the closing of a sale is often accompanied by an emotional high for your new customer. This is a wonderful time to ask for referrals.

As you are preparing to close the meeting, you might say, "Mr. Customer, thank you for your order. I know you'll be pleased with your new (product or service). Let me ask you, can you recommend anyone else who might need one?" When he offers a name, say, "Great, thank you. Could I trouble you for his phone number?" If he gives you more than one number, ask, "Which number do you think I should call first?"

With each step, your new customer becomes more and more involved in the process and, subconsciously, more and more committed to helping you. You might now follow up with another question: "It would be really helpful if you could call and introduce me, so he won't be put off by my call. Would you be willing to do this for me?" Do not be surprised if he reaches for the telephone right then and makes the introduction on the spot.

Again, your goal should be to leave with two or three referrals.

Asking for Referrals from a Satisfied Customer

If you have done a good job of servicing your customer after the sale, you can be confident you now have a satisfied customer—one who will buy from you again and who represents a potential source of excellent referrals.

Contact your satisfied customer and begin the conversation by inquiring if he is happy with his purchase and if there is anything more you can do for him. If he makes a request, then treat this as a customer service call. If not, say to him, "I'm so pleased you're enjoying your new (product or service). Can you put me in touch with anyone else who would appreciate the same experience that you are enjoying using it?"

The wonderful thing about highly satisfied customers is they often want their relatives and friends and associates to share their experience. Think of the last time you thoroughly enjoyed a movie. Didn't you want to immediately tell the closest people in your life to be sure to see it? Or recall an occasion when you were delighted or even amazed by the delicious food and quality of service at a new restaurant. Did you recommend it to others?

Beyond a doubt, there is no better source of referrals than a highly satisfied customer. But, unlike with a great movie or a fabulous new restaurant, don't expect him to pick up the phone and start calling friends and associates. It is up to you to initiate the referral-building process. And even if your customer were to recommend you to another, the odds of this person getting in touch with you would be remote at best. The initiative must come from you. You must ask for the referral.

The Follow-Up

You've asked for and received the referrals you want. Now you must follow up with that referral.

Sending a Thank-You Note to the Source

Within one day of receiving the referral, drop a quick note to your customer, thanking him for his recommendation and again reassuring him that you will treat his friend with respect. This is an important part of cementing your relationship and will pay dividends in the future in the form of repeat business and further referrals.

Reporting Back to the Source

After you have followed up with the referral, be sure to call your customer. Again, thank him for the introduction and report your results. Remember, the referral is someone who is meaningful to your customer, so he will naturally be interested in what happens.

This step is a demonstration of good manners, but it is also more. First, if you succeeded in selling to your customer's friend, he will be open to your asking him if he knows anyone else whom you might contact. Second, if you were unable to close the sale, your customer might choose to contact his friend to find out why and to reiterate his own pleasure in using your product. Either way, you stand to gain.

Sending a Gift to the Source

A further way to express your gratitude and to reinforce your relationship with your customer is to send him a gift after you have closed a sale with a referral he provided. Your gift should be appropriate to the size of the sale.

A word of caution: Regardless of the size and dollar value of your gift, be sure that it is of fine quality, for it will be a direct reflection on you and your taste.

Several years ago, we learned an important lesson. Our custom was—and still is—to send fruit baskets as thank-you gifts. On one occasion, our gift was returned to us within a matter of days. An accompanying handwritten note explained that the food was of such inferior quality that the recipient would not share it with her fellow employees. She graciously thanked us for our kind thoughts and explained that she was sure we would want to know what we were getting for our money. When we examined the package, we were shocked. The basket was beautifully decorated, but the contents consisted of a variety of cheap crackers, some nuts, and a few stale apples. Our gift to her—and its subsequent return—turned out to be a gift to us. We searched for an alternate supplier and found a company, Harry & David, that stringently monitors the quality of its offerings, just as we do our own. While their packaging is attractive, their emphasis is on a variety of beautiful fresh fruits and delectable nuts and top-quality biscuits. Since making the change, we have received countless calls and cards from very satisfied customers thanking us for our generosity!

Making Yourself Referable

We have laid out a number of tried and proven strategies for building a pipeline of referrals. The foundation upon which they must be laid, the glue that holds them all together, is you. In the final analysis, it is your character, your commitment to excellence, and your genuine concern for your customer that will determine the number and the quality of referrals your customer brings to you. Every day, look in the mirror and ask, "Am I the kind of person I would recommend to my family, to my closest friends, to my most esteemed associates?" If the answer is yes, you are on track. If not, redouble your resolve to become that kind of person. You will be happier for it. You will also enjoy unparalleled success in developing a strong referral network.

Leave no stone unturned in your efforts to develop a golden chain of referrals. Use every strategy possible to transform your customers into advocates for you, your business, and your services and products. It is the wisest and most cost-effective marketing strategy you could possibly design.

Application Exercise

1. Why would someone choose to refer you to the people he values most?

2. Why would someone choose to refer your company to the people she values most?

3. Why would your customers choose to refer your product or service to the people they value most?

4. Make a list of the customers you believe you have "delighted." They represent the most likely candidates to approach for referrals.

5. Make a list of the customers you believe you have "amazed." They, too, represent the most likely candidates to approach for referrals.

6. Devise a strategy to secure as many quality referrals as possible from your existing customer base.

7. What actions do you commit to take immediately as a result of insights gained in this chapter?

"Knowing is not enough;
we must apply.
Willing is not enough;
we must do."

JOHANN WOLFGANG VON GOETHE

CHAPTER 18

Create a Powerful Marketing Plan

"Perseverance is more prevailing than violence, and many things that cannot be overcome when they are together yield themselves up when taken little by little."

PLUTARCH

Do you have a thorough understanding of the product, price, people, and promotional options for your organization or business? YES ☐ NO ☐

Does the marketing plan for your organization or business focus the right level of attention and energy on product, price, people, and promotion? YES ☐ NO ☐

· ·

This chapter looks at the first four elements of the marketing plan—product, price, people, and promotion—and shows you how to analyze these critical aspects of your organization or business for maximum return on your marketing dollar. The Application Exercise at the end of this chapter leads you through a detailed analysis of these elements and positions you to take action for maximum competitive advantage.

· ·

WITHOUT A PROSPECT, there can be no sale. A well-conceived marketing plan is the way you attract prospects. There are seven basic elements to be taken into account when designing your marketing plan:

1. Product

2. Price

3. People

4. Promotion

5. Packaging

6. Positioning

7. Place

These seven elements are universal; they are applicable in every industry and every business. They are also closely interconnected. A single change in one can dramatically change your sales and your profitability.

In this chapter, we will focus on the first four marketing elements. The last three will be addressed in the following chapter.

Product

In creating a marketing plan, you must first be absolutely clear about your product (or service). Exactly what do you sell?

A common mistake made by many businesses is to define their product in terms of what it is. "We manufacture photocopying equipment," or "We specialize in the sale of computers and related products," or "We offer a wide array of legal services," or "We sell women's clothing." But people do not decide to purchase from you based on what you are selling; rather, they look for what your product will do for them. First, they must have a perceived need. Second, they must be convinced that your product will fill this need more easily and economically than your competitors' offering.

Ask yourself this question: "What need is satisfied by my product?" Stated differently, you might ask, "What problem does my product solve?" or "What pain does my product remove?"

For example, the retail store specializing in women's clothing might define its product as follows: "We help women look their best by matching them with their perfect wardrobe." or "We help women accelerate their careers by assisting them in choosing the ideal business apparel." or "We help brides look their most beautiful on their wedding day by designing the bridal ensemble just right for them."

Always define your product in terms of the benefits it offers the consumer. The most beautifully designed product, the most brilliantly crafted service, will sell only if it fills a perceived need.

Price

The second element of your marketing strategy is price.

What do you charge for your product? How did you arrive at this price? Is your price competitive with other products in the marketplace?

How elastic is the price of your product? In other words, how much room do you have to increase or decrease your price without impacting your ability to sell?

In addition to how much you charge, pay close attention to how you receive payment. Do you accept credit card payments? Is this important to your potential customers? What about personal checks? If you ship product, do you require payment in advance, or will you ship and bill later? Do you levy shipping charges? What about handling charges? Do you treat your shipping department as a profit center?

All of these questions must be carefully considered within the context of the marketplace. Remember, the prime determinant of your price is your competition. Revisit the competitive analysis you performed in Chapter 3. Examine your competitors' pricing models. Be sure yours is competitive.

People

The third element of your marketing strategy is people. Consider all people involved in the sales process.

First, study your customer. Create a profile of your existing customer base. If you are starting your business and have no customers as yet, your profile might describe the customers of your competitors, including their age range, gender, job, financial status, purchasing power, and so on. What kind of publications do they read? Where are they most likely to shop? What clubs and organizations might they be expected to join? What kind of job or profession are they likely to have? What other characteristics or habits are relevant to your marketing efforts?

Next, paint a picture of your ideal customer. Based on the same parameters you used in creating your existing customer profile, describe your ideal customer in detail. This information will prove invaluable in determining how you can most readily reach him and convert him into an actual customer.

Next, examine your salespeople. Perhaps it is you. Maybe you have an internal sales force, or do you sell through independent reps? It is important that whoever is interfacing with the buyer matches well to the customer profile you have just defined, otherwise he will be unable to create rapport, an essential ingredient in the sales process. It is not unusual to find women in sales positions in upscale men's clothing stores. On the other hand, men rarely sell fine clothing to women but are the norm in the heavy equipment industry. Are you and/or your salespeople the ideal match for your ideal customer?

Finally, look at your customer support people. Are they

right for the job? Do they have the proper attitude and the necessary skills? As with your salespeople, are they well suited to deal with the kind of person you have defined as your ideal customer?

Taking the time to know your customer and to ensure you have the best people in the critical positions of sales and customer service will yield great benefits to you and your business as you move forward with your marketing efforts.

Promotion

The fourth element of your marketing strategy is promotion. With the benefit of clarity regarding your product, price, and people, you can now turn your attention to how you will promote your product.

One promotional option is traditional advertising. This is an area that must be carefully analyzed from a cost-benefit perspective. While advertising can be very expensive, it can also be an effective way to raise awareness of your product. Selecting the most appropriate medium is, therefore, of paramount importance.

Perhaps the oldest advertising medium is print. Would your ideal customer be more likely to read your ad in the newspaper or a magazine, or perhaps a trade journal or on the Internet? Be sure your have a good copywriter, experienced with the medium, create your ad. This is important because, for example, the rules for writing good Web copy are different from those for print.

Consider the benefits of advertising on radio or even TV. If you opt for the broadcast media, it is important to choose the best time of day as well as the best day of the week. The type of program during which you advertise must match your ideal customer profile. As with print media, have a professional create your commercials.

Have you considered marketing on the Internet? If so, again work with a specialist who knows how to optimize a marketing message for online media as opposed to more traditional media. Maria Veloso's *Web Copy That Sells* is a good source.

In some cases, a carefully targeted direct mail campaign can be very effective. Lists can be purchased from many sources. The quality of the list—in terms of currency of information, validity of addresses, and specificity of targets—is of paramount importance. It is well worth paying a higher price per name in order to ensure fewer pieces are returned because of an incorrect address and to optimize the chances of reaching a qualified prospect.

Telemarketing is another option. In the early years of the twenty-first century, some countries are attempting to pass laws limiting this growing industry, but it is unlikely telemarketing will disappear.

In some cases, your marketing plan might include more than one promotional strategy. One of our coaching clients is a financial planner who offers investment products to senior citizens and whose most effective promotion involves presenting free seminars on the subject. In the three weeks preceding such an event, he uses radio commercials, newspaper ads, and direct mail to enroll his seminars. His ads and direct mail pieces are carefully crafted to induce only seniors with a minimum net worth of $1.5 million to attend. In addition to offering real value, his seminars also afford him the opportunity to establish enormous credibility with the audience. At the end of his presentation, he urges anyone who is interested in a free portfolio analysis to fill out a brief form, which provides him with a list of prequalified prospects. His support staff follows up and sets up meetings between him and these potential customers. His closing ratio is one of the highest in the industry.

Before blindly deciding on a marketing strategy that may prove to be both expensive and ineffective, take the time to fully understand your product, your price, your people, and your promotional options. This upfront investment of time and energy can save you countless dollars down the road. It will certainly form a foundation upon which to begin building a sound marketing strategy to aggressively grow your business in a cost-effective manner.

Application Exercise

Product

1. Describe your primary product or service in terms of what it is.

2. Describe your product or service in terms of what it does; the need(s) it fills; the pain(s) it alleviates; and the benefit(s) the customer enjoys.

3. How might you modify your product or service to better fill your customers' needs?

Price

1. What is the price of your product or service?

2. Do you offer any discounts or rebates?

3. What is the pricing of competitive products?

4. What forms of payment do you accept (i.e., cash, checks, specific credit cards)?

5. If you ship product, what are your shipping and billing policies?

6. What are the main differences between your pricing model and that of your main competitors?

7. How might you change your pricing model to become more competitive?

People

1. Describe in detail the characteristics of your existing customers.

2. Describe in detail the characteristics of your ideal customer.

3. In what ways are your sales representatives and customer service personnel compatible with your ideal customer?

4. In what ways are your sales representatives and customer service personnel not compatible with your ideal customer?

5. What changes might you make in your sales representatives and customer service personnel to better sell your product or service your customers?

Promotion

1. What are your primary means of promoting your product or service?

2. How might you promote your product differently to become more competitive in the marketplace?

Take Action

What actions do you commit to take immediately as a result of insights gained in this chapter?

"Customer focus is the key
to marketing success."

ANONYMOUS

CHAPTER 19

Complete Your Powerful Marketing Plan

"In the world of marketing, perception is everything."

ANONYMOUS

Do you have a solid and up-to-date understanding of the packaging, positioning, and place options for your organization or business? **YES ☐ NO ☐**

Does your organization or business invest the appropriate amounts of energy and resources to ensure the best packaging, positioning, and place for its products or services? **YES ☐ NO ☐**

This chapter explores the second group of key characteristics of a solid marketing plan: packaging, positioning, and place. These critical elements of the marketing plan can give your business's product or service the best possible exposure and competitive advantage. The Application Exercise at the end of this chapter takes you through the steps to complete your marketing plan while ensuring that your business gets the best possible return for its efforts.

MANAGING THE CUSTOMER'S PERCEPTION is the
critical consideration in creating a powerful marketing plan.
Successful companies focus not only on improving the economic value of their products but also on increasing their
perceived value.

Packaging

Packaging plays a major role in determining how the customer views your product. Packaging takes many forms.

First, consider the actual physical packaging, from the
product's color and shape and style to the container in which
it is shipped. Apple Computer, Inc. has been a leader in de-

signing computer shells that look sleek and modern. An Apple computer virtually shouts, "Look at me. I'm the latest and greatest!" Apple's target customers are individuals seeking the ultimate in user-friendliness and creative professionals, such as graphic designers or architects. These are the very people to whom the ultramodern packaging is most likely to appeal.

Second, the appearance of your marketing collaterals is also extremely important. If you are in the upscale clothing business, you will want all of your brochures and catalogs to have an elegant, expensive appearance. They will probably be in four-color and printed on glossy paper, showing chic models dressed in the latest fashions. On the other hand, if you run a chain of stores selling work clothes to farmers and ranchers, you will want to project a totally different image.

Third, consider the importance of personal packaging. If you are selling financial services, you want to look conservative and affluent, projecting the image of someone who is both trustworthy and successful. This will be reflected in your dress, your manner of speech, the car you drive, and so on. A very different impression would be required if you were selling motorcycles, sporting goods, or gardening equipment. Pay close attention to the image you project. It should send this clear message to your ideal customer: "Look, you can trust me. We're birds of a feather. I relate to you and your needs, and I am the right person to satisfy them."

Positioning

A vital consideration in any marketing plan is how you position yourself and your product vis-à-vis your competition.

With what you know about your ideal customer, how can you best appeal to her? What can you say or do to drown out all of the other commercial messages vying for her attention? What is the customer's hot button—and how can you push it?

At the heart of these questions is your understanding of why the potential buyer would purchase your product. What is her perceived need, and why is your product best able to satisfy it? When you have answered this question, position your product accordingly.

Is the prospect looking for quality above all else? Then position yourself as the supplier of the best-performing, longest-lasting product.

Is the buyer seeking speed of delivery? Position yourself as offering the fastest turnaround in the market.

Is price of paramount importance? Then position yourself as the lowest-cost provider.

Whatever the need, you can jump to the head of the line by positioning yourself as the leader in this area.

Ultimately, of course, you must deliver. Remember the four levels of customer satisfaction (see Chapter 16). It can be fatal to create expectations in the mind of a customer and then fail to (at least) meet these expectations. The words of Peter Drucker should be heeded: "Under-commit and over-perform." In other words, be sure that you are able to live up to the promise created by the positioning of your product.

Place

Finally, where you sell your product can have a profound impact on your success.

For many years, IBM equipment was not sold in any retail outlet. In the late 1970s, with personal computers growing in market acceptance, the company made a strategic decision to open its own retail stores, carrying chiefly IBM products and representing the only place these products could be purchased. As more and more stores offering a wide array of computer equipment and accessories became fashionable, IBM was forced to reassess its strategy. The result is that today, IBM equipment is available through many competing retail outlets alongside most of its major competitors' products.

In the past, doctors made house calls. Today, if you want to see your doctor, there is a high probability you will have to go to his office. Depending on the patient (i.e., customer profile), the office décor will vary widely—homey and comfortable with a plethora of toys and children's books in the case of an obstetrician, to severe or even spartan in the case of a radiologist.

Lawyers specializing in corporate law who deal primarily with large corporations are normally located in downtown high-rise office buildings, and their office décor is usually tasteful, elegant, and expensive. Smaller law firms might be located in suburban areas with less ostentatious offices.

Every effort should be made to ensure that the location where you conduct business is convenient for your customers. The facility should be appointed in a fashion that will make a customer feel comfortable. Strive to make it as easy and as inviting as possible for customers to do business with you.

The Internet is fast becoming an indispensable and ever more important location to conduct business. It is one of the fastest-growing marketing channels. Does your product lend itself to marketing on the Internet? If so, do you have a Web site? Has it been professionally designed? Have you taken the same pains to tailor its appearance to appeal to your ideal customer, just as you have with your office décor? Does your site have e-commerce capability? Do you have someone on staff, or perhaps an outside contractor, who stays abreast of changes in technology to update your site accordingly? Do you, or an employee or outside contractor, specialize in the business—as opposed to the technology—of your Web site? Have you developed a marketing plan for your Web site? If you do not keep abreast of Internet developments, you will run the risk of being left behind—a relic in a progressive world.

As you move forward in completing and implementing your marketing plan, be sure to carefully consider the final three Ps of marketing: packaging, positioning, and place. Combined with product, price, people, and promotion (covered in Chapter 18), they form the matrix of a powerful marketing initiative.

Application Exercise

Packaging

1. What are the ways you could package your product differently to make it more attractive and more competitive?

2. What kinds of changes could you make to the appearance of your marketing collaterals to make them more attractive and more appealing to your ideal customer?

3. How might you alter your personal image and/or that of your employees who interact with the public to create a more favorable impression with your ideal customer?

Positioning

1. What is the primary need or concern of your ideal customer?

2. How can you position your product to address this need or concern?

3. Are you able to deliver on the inherent promise in such a positioning strategy?

4. If not, what steps will you take to ensure that you "under-commit and over-perform"?

Place

1. Where do you sell your product?

2. How might you change your location to become more competitive?

3. How might you change your décor to become more competitive?

4. How might you change your Internet strategy to become more competitive?

Take Action

What actions do you commit to take immediately as a result of insights gained in this chapter?

"The will to win is important,
but the will to prevail is vital."

JOE PATERNO

CHAPTER 20

Create Your Personal Brand

"There is more credit and satisfaction in being a first-rate truck driver than a tenth-rate executive."

B. C. FORBES

Have you consciously created a personal brand that accurately reflects the person you are, or the person you are committed to becoming? YES ☐ NO ☐

Is your personal brand reflected in the promises you make (the image you project) and the promises you keep?   YES ☐ NO ☐

This chapter explores the powerful role of personal branding in building a career or business. Learn how the promises you make and the promises you keep can generate huge benefits for you and your organization or business. The seven laws of personal branding offer a blueprint for pulling together every aspect of your professional life and communicating your true value to colleagues and customers. The Application Exercise at the end of the chapter will help you analyze the elements of your personal brand and pull them together for the greatest possible impact.

JUST AS SURELY AS BUILDING a powerful corporate brand is the key to differentiating a product in the marketplace, and thus building a successful business, so creating a strong personal brand is the key to differentiating yourself from your competitors, thereby ensuring your own success as well as that of your business. Your personal brand determines how people respond to you, whether they listen to you, whether they buy from you, how much they buy, what they are willing to pay, and so on.

You may be surprised to learn that you are your most important product. As such, you already have your own personal brand. You might think of it as your image or your reputation. It is how people perceive you; the values, virtues, qualities, and attributes they ascribe to you. It is not a question of whether you should have a personal brand image, for you already have one. Rather, it is a question of whether you choose to consciously create your personal brand or merely leave it to chance.

If you are running a small entrepreneurial business, your personal brand will have as much influence over the success of your business as will your corporate brand. You should very carefully think through how you would like people to think about you, and then make sure everything you say and do is consistent with this image.

Create and Build Your Personal Brand

There are two elements of personal branding: the promises you make (i.e., the image you project) and the promises you keep (i.e., your reputation).

Promises You Make

Your personal brand makes a promise: "If you buy from me, you will receive a specific value in return." This promised value will be born from the values, virtues, qualities, and attributes by which you become known. For example, you may want to create a personal image—a brand—of a person who always operates at a high level of integrity, consistently walks the talk, is an exemplary leader, and goes the extra mile to ensure customer satisfaction.

Your decision as to precisely how to brand yourself will have two bases. First, it must be an accurate picture of the person you are, or the person you are committed to becoming. Second, it must reflect the kind of person who will elicit in a prospective customer a strong response: "I want to do business with this woman or man." In other words, your personal brand should reduce or eliminate any sense of risk in dealing with you in the mind of the buyer.

Who is your ideal customer? What values, virtues, qualities, and attributes will he be looking for in a supplier of your product? Do you match this profile? If not, do you have a burning desire to be this kind of person? Are you committed to transforming yourself into this kind of person? These are the key questions you must ask yourself when beginning to build your personal brand.

Be brutally honest with yourself. In any relationship, to try to fake who you are is a recipe for failure. To be authentic is to create trust in all of your relationships, both personal and professional.

Promises You Keep

As we stress throughout our coaching program, unmet expectations are the arch enemy of any relationship. This is no less true in the relationship between you and your customers. Your brand as a person is determined in large part by whether you consistently deliver on your promises. Do you keep your word? Do you follow up? Do your words and actions match with the image you want to create—that is, with the values, virtues, qualities, and attributes you claim as your own?

Constantly examine your behavior. When you slip, resolve to get back on track. To build and sustain a powerful personal brand, your message must be an accurate reflection of you, the messenger.

The Whole Package

Pay close attention to your entire image. Of course, your character is of paramount importance. But you make an impact on people in other ways as well.

Your appearance—the clothes you wear, your personal grooming, your posture—has an enormous emotional impact on how other people see you, think about you, and relate to you.

Your attitude is vital. If you are genuinely pleasant and cheerful in your interaction with others, they will enjoy being with you. They will be more inclined to trust you and do business with you.

Your overall behavior strongly influences the impression others have of you. Be punctual for meetings and appointments. Be absolutely reliable, always keeping your word and your commitments. Should you fail in this area, communicate with the other person as quickly as possible, offering your apology, explanation, and assurance that it will not happen again. Be responsive to the needs of your customers. Get back to them promptly. Develop a sense of urgency. Become a "Do it now" kind of person. Develop the reputation of being the "Go to" person when a customer has a problem or needs something done quickly and well.

Pay close attention to the quality of your work. In the long run, there is nothing that will so determine your success in building and sustaining a powerful personal brand as turning out high-quality work, over and over again and over a long period of time.

There are seven laws of personal branding you must master, if you are to drive your business to new levels of excellence and profitability.

The Seven Laws of Personal Branding

1. *The Law of Specialization.* Focus your brand on one specific area of achievement in your work. Avoid diversification. Do not try to be all things to all people. Select a specific industry, product, service, or skill in which you can excel.

2. *The Law of Leadership.* Become one of the most knowledgeable, skilled, and respected people in your field. Be the very best at what you do. Consistently strive to become better and better.

3. *The Law of Personality.* Your personal brand must be built around your personality, in all its aspects. The most important part of personal branding is that you be perceived as a nice and trustworthy person. Be pleasant, positive, and cheerful. Treat everyone well, no matter what the circumstances. And always do what you say you will do. Be sure your customers enjoy their interaction with you and know they can depend on you.

4. *The Law of Distinctiveness.* Once you have created your own personal brand, you must express it in a unique way. Everything you do must be part of the "package." Sometimes a small factor, like sending cookies to a customer, can brand you in a distinct way. Why? Because no one else does it. Your goal is to be perceived as unique, thus differentiating you from everyone else vying for the attention of your prospective customer.

5. *The Law of Visibility.* To be effective, your personal brand must be seen repeatedly and consistently. You

must be busy and active. Join business associations in your industry and attend meetings. Introduce yourself and hand out business cards. When you call on a customer, introduce yourself to other people in the office. The more you are seen in a positive way, the more powerful your personal brand will be.

6. *The Law of Congruence.* Your behavior must be consistent, both publicly and privately. Everything you do behind closed doors should be consistent with what you do in public. People should feel that there is complete alignment or congruence between the public person and the private person. And both must be authentic, not merely a false persona adopted for the purpose of impressing or manipulating others.

7. *The Law of Persistence.* Once you have built your personal brand, you must now sustain it. Never deviate from it. Give it time to grow. Stick with your personal brand through thick and thin until it sets like hardened cement in the minds of other people.

The time and energy you invest in building a powerful, positive, personal brand will pay huge dividends. People will trust you and willingly accept your suggestions and recommendations. They will buy from you more readily, again and again, and even pay more for your products and services than for those of your competitors. They will gladly provide you with referrals, open doors for you, and create opportunities not available to others. A positive personal brand will enable you to more readily secure credit and borrow money.

Remember, "Everything counts!" Everything you do either enhances or detracts from your brand. Every word you utter either adds to or takes away from the quality of your personal brand. Your responsibility is to ensure that everything you do and say is consistent with the perception you want others to have of you. This is the key to building a powerful, positive, personal brand.

Resolve today to pay the price. You will be richly rewarded for your efforts.

Application Exercise

1. What words do people use when describing you?

2. What words do you want people to use when describing you?

3. Why will a personal brand, based on this image you project, compel your ideal customer to buy from you?

4. What promises do you make—that is, what value does a customer expect to receive when she buys your product or service?

5. Do you deliver on your promises?

6. What changes might you make in your values, attitudes, and behavior in order to be congruent with your desired image or personal brand?

7. What actions do you commit to take immediately as a result of insights gained in this chapter?

"There is no such thing as a good excuse."

DERO AMES SAUNDERS

CHAPTER 21

Maximize Profits

"Sometimes you must fight and win, just because all the pain and suffering you experienced up to this point on your quest would be rendered futile if you were to surrender now."

ALVIN DAY

Within the last six months, have you assessed the profitability of your organization or your business? **YES** ☐ **NO** ☐

Can you identify the profitability of the following six elements in your organization or business: Employees? Customers? Sales and marketing efforts? Products and services? Markets? Yourself (as measured by your tasks and activities)? **YES** ☐ **NO** ☐

This chapter shows you how to assess the profitability of your organization or business by examining those six key elements. The Application Exercise at the end of this chapter will help you identify the weak links in the chain of profitability so that you can take appropriate action to ensure that every aspect of your organization or business contributes to generating the highest possible profits.

185

OVER THE PAST SIX CHAPTERS, you have mastered a variety of strategies aimed at increasing the sales of your business.

Sales vs. Profits

However, sales are only one barometer of success. Your ultimate goal is to increase profits in order to achieve the greatest possible return on your investment of money, time, and energy.

Every customer, activity, product, or service yields a specific profit of a specific amount. In some cases, you may actually be losing money in one or more of these areas. One of the most important things you can do in growing your business is to determine where to focus the investment of your time and money based on the return thrown off by this investment.

Personal Profitability

To truly analyze the profitability of your business, you must first examine your personal rate of return.

From this personal perspective, what is your major expense? It is your time. In Part II of this book, where we explored how to increase productivity, we examined the importance of your hourly rate—your annual income divided by 2,000. By now, you should have developed the habit of continually asking yourself this basic question: Would I pay someone else my hourly rate to perform this task? If not, you are failing to maximize the return on your time. In other words, you are investing your time in an area that yields less than the optimum rate of return. You are incurring a "loss of opportunity" cost. This, in turn, affects the overall profitability of your business.

Instill this discipline in the culture of your organization. Like you, your people should develop the habit of "return on time" thinking.

The basic rule is this: Perform only those tasks for which you would pay someone else your hourly rate (or more); eliminate or delegate the rest.

People Profitability

Payroll represents one of the largest expense items for most businesses. As a business grows, it typically hires additional staff according to the most pressing need at the moment. Once a person has been hired, often she or he can become a permanent fixture, even when needs change. Many entrepreneurs are too busy creating products, designing services, and generating revenues to pay close attention to employee performance. Over time, the result can be an inefficient and ineffective staff and a bloated payroll.

From an accounting perspective, payroll is an expense. We regard it as an investment and, as such, it must yield at least an acceptable rate of return. But the goal should be an optimal return. What is acceptable or optimal? And how can it be measured? This varies by industry and even by size of company. A general rule of thumb is that each employee should contribute three to six times her salary in gross revenues. Stated differently, revenues in your business should be three to six times your payroll. And if you head up your own small business, don't forget to include yourself in this calculation. Although you may not draw a salary, you still represent a cost to the business. If you were not there, how much would you have to pay someone else to perform your role? A common mistake made by many entrepreneurs is to forget the cost of their own input when calculating the profitability of their business.

Customer Profitability

As we have discussed, some customers are more profitable than others. Some may actually be costing you money. Can you identify your most profitable customers? Do you know any who are unprofitable? There is not necessarily any connection between the size of a customer or the volume of business he produces and his profitability.

There are several questions you should ask as you examine your customer profitability:

How often does each customer purchase from you?
What is the average size of each purchase?
What is the profit margin of the product(s) purchased?
How much time is spent in providing customer service after the sale?
What is the "product returns" record of each customer?

As in so many other areas, you might find that Pareto's Law applies: Twenty percent of your customers may account for 80 percent of your profits. The question becomes, what do you do with your least profitable customers?

Many companies regularly "fire" the bottom 10 percent of their customers. They stop doing business with those who generate the least revenues or yield the lowest return on their purchases, choosing to concentrate on their more profitable customers and attracting more like them. At the very least, be diligent in rooting out those customers who actually cost you money—regardless of the revenues they generate. You cannot afford to carry this unprofitable load.

Sales and Marketing Profitability

Do you know the return on your sales and marketing expenditures? It is not unusual for companies to spend 25 percent to 35 percent of their revenues on sales and marketing, yet often they do not know the actual return on these initiatives.

One of our clients, the owner of a small print shop, was determined to increase his revenue base by 50 percent within one year. A marketing consultant convinced our client to mount an aggressive and costly direct mail campaign. Sure enough, within eleven months his revenues were up by an impressive 56 percent. Unfortunately, his year-end financial statements showed a loss—his first unprofitable year in over ten years in business. He had surpassed his sales goals, but the cost of acquiring this new business exceeded the profits generated by these additional sales. The return on his direct mail campaign was negative, and he immediately abandoned it.

Before adopting a new marketing initiative, determine how you will measure not only its impact on sales but on profits as well. What is an acceptable rate of return on this marketing expense? What is an optimal return? How will you measure the return? Do not wait until the marketing effort has been completed. Establish a monitoring system whereby you can gauge the efficacy of the program throughout its implementation.

Examine your existing sales and marketing expenses. Do you know the return on these dollars? If not, find out! Increasing sales is a wonderful goal but not at the expense of the bottom line.

Product Profitability

As we stated at the beginning of this chapter, every product yields a specific profit of a specific amount. When you offer more than one product, each will have its own profit margin. One of the most important things you can do is to determine the return on the investment you have put into each of your products.

Marathon and Associates, a niche consulting firm, receives enormous fees from Fortune 1000 companies to determine the exact cost of each of their products. This enables their clients to make product-offering decisions based on the profitability of each product, rather than simply relying on gross revenue figures. In today's highly competitive business climate, such an approach is critical in ensuring their overall profitability and even their survival. This is no less true of your own business or organization. Eliminating just one losing product can make the difference between robust growth and mediocre performance or even the demise of your business.

Examine your own product mix. In addition to the normal "cost of goods," you must include all expenses incurred in delivering the finished product to the consumer, including research and development, promotion, associated sales and marketing costs, installation, customer service, product service, returns, proportionate share of general and administrative costs (overhead), and so on. Again, be sure to include the cost of your own time; apply your hourly rate to the amount of time you invest in the development, design, creation/manufacture, sale, and servicing of the product.

Many individuals and businesses lump all their expenses together and then guess at how much is attributable to each product. Your job is to break your costs down so accurately that you know within a few dollars exactly how much you net from the sale of each product.

When you have completed your costing analysis, simply deduct the actual cost of developing, selling, and delivering each product from the price to determine its profitability. Which products yield the highest return? The lowest? Do any actually lose money?

Market Profitability

If you sell into more than one market, the same principle applies. Some markets will be more profitable than others.

When dealing in foreign markets, for example, you may incur much higher advertising and marketing costs. Conversely, your manufacturing costs might be significantly lower. If you export your products into foreign countries, import duties or tariffs may apply.

At times, unexpected costs in dealing in new markets may make the difference between a profitable venture and a financial disaster. An independent distributor of home electronic goods based in the United States decided to enter the Canadian market. He was shocked to learn that, in order to sell in the province of Quebec, he would have to redesign his packaging to feature French as well as English. Considering the size of the market, the additional cost was prohibitive, and as a result, he decided to abandon the entire Canadian venture. It pays to do your homework upfront!

Examine your markets by asking:

Are some markets more profitable than others?
Do some require higher advertising and promotion budgets in order to reach your sales targets?
Is there a difference in terms of product returns?
What are the customer service costs after the sale?
Do you incur any additional shipping costs, tariffs, or other extraneous expenses when you sell into markets beyond your locale?

Take Action

Based on your various profitability studies, you are now in a position to make decisions and take action.

What will you do with employees who are not carrying their weight? Establish benchmarks they must meet, and provide the necessary training and support to help them do so. If they fail, set them free.

Get rid of your unprofitable customers, regardless of the amount of revenues they generate. Give serious thought to pruning the 10 percent who yield the lowest profits, directing the resources they have been absorbing toward attracting higher-profit customers.

Take a close look at your money-losing and low-profit products. Quickly explore ways to make them profitable or to increase their margins. Can you raise prices? Can you reduce costs? Can you change your offering to attract more buyers, thereby spreading costs across a larger number of products? Do not make the all-too-common mistake of falling in love with any product. Even if it is a best-seller, if you cannot bring it up to an acceptable profit level, eliminate it.

Even though they may be diligent in tracking the profitability of their products, many businesses do not differentiate between markets. Do not fall into this trap. If a market or submarket does not yield an acceptable level of profits, explore how you might raise the profitability in this area. Can you raise prices? Can you pass shipping costs on to the buyer? Is there a way to cut costs in the lagging market? If you fail to raise the profitability of a particular market to reach your targets, abandon it.

As you continue to grow your business by driving sales, remember that the critical measure of success in any business is profits. Develop the habit of regularly examining the profitability of your people, your customers, your sales and marketing initiatives, your products, and your markets. If underperformers cannot be brought up to your standards, waste no time in getting rid of them. This discipline alone will make you one of the most successful businesses in your field.

Application Exercise

1. Identify your most and your least profitable/productive tasks and activities.

2. Identify your most and your least profitable employees.

3. Identify are your most and your least profitable customers.

4. Identify your most and your least profitable marketing initiatives.

5. Identify your most and your least profitable products/services.

6. Identify your most and your least profitable markets.

7. Identify the actions you will commit to take immediately as a result of insights gained in this chapter.

"Never give in, never give in, never, never, never, never—in nothing, great or small, large or petty—never give in except to convictions of honor and good sense."

WINSTON CHURCHILL

List of Values

Accuracy
Action
Adaptability
Adventure
Affection
Alertness
Ambition
Assertiveness
Authenticity

Balance
Beauty
Boldness
Broad-mindedness

Calmness
Career-focus
Caring
Cautiousness

Clear-headedness
Compassion
Competence
Confidence
Conscientious
Considerate
Contribution
Cooperation
Courage
Creativity

Dependability
Determination
Diligence
Dynamic

Education
Effectiveness

Energy
Enjoyment
Enterprise
Enthusiasm
Excellence

Faith
Flexibility
Focus
Forgiveness
Freedom
Friendliness
Fulfillment

Generosity
Gentleness
Growth

Happiness
Health

197

Helpfulness
Honesty
Hope
Humility
Humor

Imagination
Impartiality
Independence
Innovation
Integrity
Intelligence

Joviality
Joyfulness

Kindness
Knowledge

Leadership
Learning
Love
Loyalty

Maturity
Method

Meticulousness
Modesty

Naturalness
Nurturing

Optimism
Organization
Originality

Patience
Peace
Perseverance
Persistence
Playfulness
Pleasant
Polite
Positive Mental
    Attitude
Possessiveness
Practical
Precision
Professionalism
Progress
Prosperity

Punctuality
Purposefulness

Quality
Quickness

Resourcefulness
Respect
Responsibility

Self-Control
Sensibility
Sensitivity
Sincerity
Sociability
Specialness
Strength

Tact
Talent
Teamwork
Thankfulness
Thoroughness
Tolerance
Trustworthiness

Understanding	Victory	Wisdom
Uniqueness	Vigor	Wit
		Youthfulness
Value	Warmth	
Versatility	Willpower	Zeal

Advanced Coaching and Mentoring Program

Brian Tracy offers a personal coaching program in San Diego for successful entrepreneurs, self-employed professionals, and top salespeople.

Participants learn a step-by-step process of personal strategic planning that enables them to take complete control of their time and their lives. Over the course of the program, participants meet with Brian Tracy one full day every three months. During these sessions, they learn how to double their income and double their time off. Participants learn how to apply this "Focal Point" process to every part of their work and personal lives.

They identify the things they enjoy doing the most and learn how to become better in their most profitable activities. Participants learn how to delegate, downsize, eliminate, and get rid of all the tasks they neither enjoy nor benefit from. They learn how to identify their special talents and how to use leverage and concentration to move to the top of their fields.

For more information on the Coaching and Mentoring Program, visit http://www.briantracy.com, call 858-481-2977, or write to Brian Tracy International, 462 Stevens Road, Solana Beach, CA, 92075.

Index

About the Authors

Brian Tracy is one of America's top business speakers, a best-selling author, and one of the leading consultants and trainers on personal and professional development in the world today. He addresses 250,000 people each year on subjects ranging from Personal Success and Leadership to Managerial Effectiveness, Creativity, and Sales. He has written more than thirty books, and has produced more than 300 audio and video learning programs. Much of Brian's work has been translated into other languages and is being used in thirty-five countries. He is coauthor, with Campbell Fraser, of the Advanced Coaching and Mentoring Program and the Coaching Excellence Program.

Brian has consulted with more than 1000 companies—IBM, McDonnell Douglas, and The Million Dollar Round Table among them—and has trained more than 2,000,000 people personally. His ideas are proven, practical, and fast-acting. His readers, seminar participants, and coaching clients learn a series of techniques and strategies that they can use immediately to get better results in their lives and careers.

Campbell Fraser is one of the world's foremost authorities on personal and entrepreneurial coaching. He is coauthor, with Brian Tracy, of the Advanced Coaching and Mentoring

Program and the Coaching Excellence Program. He began his career as a financial analyst and venture capital specialist, and then spent twenty years building his own successful investment company. Campbell Fraser addresses audiences throughout the U.S. and worldwide on how entrepreneurs and executives can more effectively meet the challenges posed by today's rapidly changing business environment.